TREKS IN THE DOLOMITES:

ALTE VIE 1 AND 2

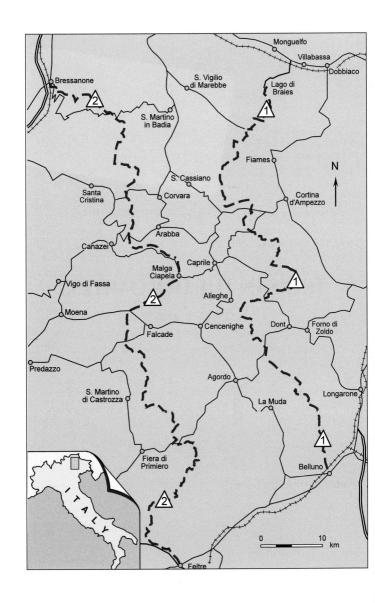

MOUNTAIN SAFETY

Every mountain walk has its dangers, and those described in this guide-book are no exception. All who walk or climb in the mountains should recognise this and take responsibility for themselves and their companions along the way. The author and publisher have made every effort to ensure that the information contained herein was correct when the guide went to press, but they cannot accept responsibility for any loss, injury or inconvenience sustained by any person using this book.

International Distress Signal
(To be used in emergency only)
Six blasts on a whistle (and flashes with a torch after dark) spaced evenly for one minute, followed by a minute's pause. Repeat until an answer is received. The response is three signals per minute followed by a minute's pause.

The following signals are used to communicate with a helicopter:

Help needed:
raise both arms above head to form a 'V'

Help not required:
raise one arm above head, extend other arm downward

Note: *mountain rescue can be very expensive – be adequately insured*

The view south from Rifugio Nuvolau, Alta Via 1

ABOUT THE AUTHORS

MARTIN COLLINS

Martin Collins is a freelance author, photo-journalist and cartographer, as well as a regular contributor to the UK outdoor media. First walking the GR5 in 1981 kindled a passion for the French Alps that remains as strong as ever. He has since written over twenty books for walkers embracing the coast, mountains and countryside of the UK and parts of Europe. He has three children, and lives in north Wales on the edge of the Snowdonia National Park.

Other Cicerone guidebooks by Martin Collins
Chamonix – Mont-Blanc
The Pennine Way
North Yorks Moors
The Teesdale Way
South West Way
A Walker's Guide to the Isle of Wight (with Norman Birch)

GILLIAN PRICE

Gillian Price was born in England and moved to Australia when young. She took a degree in anthropology and then worked in adult education before moving to Venice, which she had visited as a student and to which she had vowed to return permanently.

Gillian now lives there with her husband, Nicola, a native Venetian, and works as a writer and translator, including stints for the Venice Film Festival.

Venice is only two hours from the Dolomites. Starting there, Gillian has steadily explored the mountain ranges of Italy and brought them to life for visitors in a series of outstanding guides for Cicerone.

Other Cicerone guidebooks by Gillian Price
Walking in the Central Italian Alps
Walking in the Dolomites
Shorter Walks in the Dolomites
Walking in Italy's Gran Paradiso
Walking in Sicily
Walking in Tuscany
Walking in Corsica
Trekking in the Apennines

TREKS IN THE DOLOMITES:

ALTE VIE 1 AND 2

by
Martin Collins
and
Gillian Price

CICERONE

2 POLICE SQUARE, MILNTHORPE, CUMBRIA, LA7 7PY
www.cicerone.co.uk

© Martin Collins and Gillian Price 2002
Second edition
Reprinted 2005
(based on first edition by Martin Collins, 1986)
ISBN 1 85284 359 4

maps and profiles: Nicola Regine, based in some cases on originals by Martin Collins
illustrations: Martin Collins
photographs: Martin Collins and Gillian Price
Martin Collins: frontispiece, 13, 18, 29, 30, 31, 36, 37, 56, 58, 65, 74, 78, 80, 82, 86, 96, 98, 104, 105, 112
Gillian Price: 12, 15, 21, 23, 24, 25, 26, 27, 28, 31, 34, 35, 39, 40, 41, 42, 46, 47, 49, 50, 51, 52, 53, 59, 60, 66, 68, 79, 81, 83, 84, 85, 89, 90, 91, 92, 93, 94, 99, 106, 107, 109, 110, 111, 114, 115, 117, 126, 127
A catalogue record for this book is available from the British Library.

First edition

This book is dedicated to Diana, without whose patience and enthusiastic support it would not have been compiled. Grateful thanks are due to Jill Heslop for her assistance with the Italian language.

Second edition

Dedicated to little Gillian from Conegliano. Thanks to Nick for his great graphic work and, of course, company on the trail; Piero for a path check; and Giorgio for posing.

Advice to Readers

Readers are advised that while every effort is taken by the authors to ensure the accuracy of this guidebook, changes can occur which may affect the contents. It is advisable to check locally on transport, accommodation, shops, etc, but even rights of way can be altered.

The publisher would welcome notes of any such changes.

Front cover: Cloud-capped Monte Pelmo from the summit of the Nuvolau

CONTENTS

KEY TO MAPS

⁓ ⁓ ⁓	alta via route
··········	variant
⁓⁓⁓	motorable road
⬆	refuge
⬆	bivouac hut
▲	mountain summit
◉	town or village
⬯	lake
○—○—○	cable-car, gondola car or chair lift

INTRODUCTION

Situated towards the eastern end of the Alps' great curve from the Mediterranean coast through Central Europe to the Balkans, the Dolomites region occupies an area of northern Italy as large as Wales.

Until the Great War, the South Tyrol, which embraces the northern Dolomites, was part of the Austro-Hungarian Empire. During the bitter fighting that took place between 1914 and 1918, avalanches, mountain weather and difficult terrain added to the burden of hardship endured by Austrian and Italian troops alike. Evidence of the war is still clearly visible in the old tunnels and gun positions, discarded mess tins, boot soles and barbed wire. The 1919 Treaty of Versailles gave the South Tyrol to Italy. Its population has remained largely German-speaking, though the majority also understand Italian nowadays.

The Dolomites' name is thought to derive from that of a French geologist – the Marquis de Dolomieu – who wrote enthusiastically about the special qualities of its rock after visiting the area in 1789. The subsequent development of rock and ice climbing throughout Europe is inextricably linked with the Dolomites, many claiming that steep wall climbing – already in full swing before World War One – was born here, with pio-neers like Paul Preuss, Hans Dulfer and Angelo Dibona establishing diffi-cult routes on the vertical rock.

First ascents of the Cima Grande di Lavaredo, Monte Cristallo, the Mar-molada, Tofane and Sassolungo were achieved almost exclusively by conti-nental climbers, though John Ball, first president of the Alpine Club in Britain, reached the summit of Monte Pelmo in 1857. Artificial climbing followed on, with emerging skills and tech-niques being applied to the great but-tresses and faces of the Western Alps during the 1920s and 1930s.

Although the Dolomites' reputa-tion as a playground for 'hard men' is fully justified, these mountains are by no means the domain of the rock climber alone. A dense network of footpaths offers endless scope for exhilarating high-level walks; the renowned *vie ferrate* (rock routes aided by fixed metal ladders and cables) lead up into many sensational situations, while in winter the region becomes a premier skiing destination for thousands of Europeans.

Of relatively modest height com-pared with the giants of the Central and Western Alps, the soaring lime-stone peaks here reach, nevertheless, up to 3300m. Fairy-tale spires, broad rock plateaux, mountain lakes and plunging, forested valleys provide a

On the Sentiero delle Farangole high above Val delle Comelle (Alta Via 2)

uniquely stunning environment. Scenery, sometimes bizarre and other-worldly, is always fascinating.

At present there are seven long-distance high routes – 'Alte Vie' – comprising stretches of footpath, ancient mule tracks and military roads linked together into itineraries of special appeal to the mountain walker. This guide deals with Alta Via 1 and Alta Via 2, generally considered to be the finest and showpieces of their kind. They run on a north to south axis through the very heart of the Dolomites, connecting Tyrolean Val Pusteria with the fringes of the Veneto plain and passing through a wide variety of landscape and human upland settlements.

The walking itself varies from

level strolling to the odd scramble on rock clipped to fixed metal ropes; from long, ambling ascents in forest to steep traverses on rough scree or snow. Height is maintained throughout at about 2000– 2500m, dropping to road passes at regular intervals and reaching 2932m (over 9600ft) on Alta Via 2 – the highest point on either route.

Alte Vie 1 and 2 are of ideal length for the average walking holiday, though precise distances are hard to determine owing to innumerable zigzags, rough ground and ascents/descents. Alta Via 1 is approximately 150km (93 miles) long, while Alta Via 2 totals about 185km (115 miles).

Progress along the trail, however, is not always quick and straightforward, and it is best to allow at least 10 days for Alta Via 1, and up to 2½ weeks for Alta Via 2. Given general conditions, very fit walkers could reduce these times considerably, but to hurry through such marvellous country is to miss much. The suggested times allow for the odd excursion off route and episodes of bad weather which can upset the best laid plans.

Alta Via 1 was the first of its kind to be officially established and in many ways remains a showpiece, leading the walker into delectable mountain locations. Only the last stage, from Passo Duran to Belluno, poses any problems – easily bypassed if needs be; elsewhere there are quite lengthy and easy stretches between the higher massifs.

Alta Via 2 is longer and, on the whole, more rugged in character, climbing and dropping more in total than Alta Via 1 and staying consistently higher. Its final section from Passo Cereda to Feltre is remote, with refuges thin on the ground. For all that, it is an equally fine route, with stunning scenery culminating in the Marmolada – the highest peak in the Dolomites.

Because they are renowned and popular with Italians as well as other Europeans, Alte Vie 1 and 2 are well walked by people of all abilities. By no means everyone tackles the routes in their entirety, many preferring to take bites at the most scenic and accessible portions. The fact they can be walked in stages to suit individual needs is a major attraction of these Alte Vie. Refuges appear at regular intervals (many also reached by rough road or mechanised means), thus acting as termini to shorter walks, as well as refreshment and accommodation halts for the long-distance hiker.

The authors hope that these treks through the Dolomites will yield rewarding experiences and enduring memories for everyone visiting this most extraordinary region.

Sunset from Passo Giau (Alta Via 1)

HOW TO GET THERE

By plane, the nearest useful airports are at Verona and Venice, as well as Innsbruck in Austria and Munich in southern Germany, all with excellent ongoing train services. Otherwise, from northern Europe the Dolomites are most directly approached from Austria over the Brenner Pass. This involves using either rail links from the Channel ports or the toll-paying motorway from Innsbruck.

For Alta Via 1 change trains at Fortezza for the Brunico–Dobbiaco line along Val Pusteria and get off at Villabassa. A summer bus service runs from here to Lago di Braies, the start point. Drivers along the Val Pusteria will find the turn-off for Lago di Braies a short distance west of Villabassa.

For Alta Via 2, by road or rail, continue south from the Brenner Pass to the sizeable town of Bressanone; plenty of parking is available.

At the end of your journey through the Dolomites, it is possible to return to the start of both routes by bus/train combinations. Alternatives include hiring a taxi or driving to the end points Belluno or Feltre first, with spare clothes and other essentials left in the vehicle to look forward to!

Many points along both Alte Vie, including several refuges, are accessible from motorable roads. For walkers preferring to sample stretches of route without the commitment of leaving vehicles parked at the start of the Alta Via, the trail could be reached at such access points and a circular walk undertaken; or a driver could take the vehicle on ahead to the next access point for walkers to be met. Notes in the text and sketch maps provided will assist plans to take the walking in instalments.

Italian rail timetables tel. 892021 or www.trenitalia.com; bus timetables for South Tyrol, including Lago di Braies and Bressanone tel. toll-free 800-846047 or www.sad.it. For Feltre and Belluno buses contact Dolomiti Bus tel. 0437-941167 or www. dolomitibus.it.

MAPS AND WAYMARKING

This book contains route guides for Alte Vie nos. 1 and 2. They are broken up into stages, each of which is accompanied by a sketch map showing important features.

Walkers in this high, rugged mountain country will, however, also need to carry maps for four good reasons. First, as a vital navigational aid should the path be missed or if visibility becomes poor. Second, to allow a sensible escape route to be chosen in emergencies such as sickness or injury. Third, to help in planning lower-level alternative itineraries to avoid high, exposed stretches in bad weather. Fourth, to add pleasure to the journey by enabling the identification of features in the mountain environment – such as peaks, glaciers, cols and settlements.

Alta Via 2 waymarking

There are three principal map series covering Alte Vie nos. 1 and 2.

Tabacco offers the best, an excellent **1:25,000 series** with blue covers, 'Carta topografica per escursionisti'. Finely drawn in a clear style with contour lines every 25m and frequently updated, they contain a wealth of detail and show the Alte Vie with triangles – blue for AV1, red/orange for AV2 – and corresponding number. Sheets pertaining to AV1 are 031 (Dolomiti di Braies), 03 (Cortina d'Ampezzo), 025 (Dolomiti di Zoldo) and 024 (Prealpi e Dolomiti Bellunesi) (**note:** walkers who skip the *via ferrata* on the Schiara can do without this last map). Sheets needed for AV2 are 030 (Bressanone), 05 (Val Gardena) or 07 (Alta Badia), 015 (Marmolada), 022 (Pale di San Martino) and 023 (Alpi Feltrine).

One negative note: a recent trend to acknowledge local cultures, Ladin and otherwise, has seen the untoward introduction of dialect names on these maps, confusing at times to say the least and often at odds with local usage. For instance, instead of *Rifugio*, maps covering the Val Badia use *Ütia*, the Ladin name, as well as varied spellings for mountains. The Italian versions, more widely accepted and used, have been adhered to in this guide for simplicity.

Secondly, **Tabacco** also has an older **1:50,000 series**, which means fewer sheets are needed. Though the relief is drawn rather crudely, footpaths are overprinted clearly in red, and the Alte Vie are identified. Contours are at 50m intervals. See sheets 1 and 4 for AV1; and 9, 2 and 4 for AV2.

Thirdly, **Kompass** produce a green- and blue-covered **1:50,000**

15

'Wanderkarte' showing numbered footpaths and useful features such as refuges in red, as is common practice. Whilst just adequate, they leave a lot to be desired. Alte Vie routings are not up to date, and contours are at 100m intervals, making gradients harder to read. However, they do cover the entire area and could be used for planning in conjunction with this guide. Sheets required are nos. 57, 55 and 77 (AV1); 56, 59 and 76 (AV2).

Various hatchings and broken lines are employed to denote a footpath's difficulty: a continuous line usually indicates a broad, easy track or mountain road; a broken line a normal mountain path over mixed terrain; a dotted line a particularly steep or rough section; and a line of crosses a rock route or *via ferrata*. However there are discrepancies. Whilst a dotted line may not always prove tricky on the ground, some broken-line stretches can come as a nasty surprise.

Most of the maps mentioned can be ordered at outdoor equipment suppliers or bookshops, and can be purchased in the major cities of north Italy in addition to the Dolomite regions.

Both Alte Vie start in the predominantly German-speaking South Tyrol, but to avoid tedious repetition of place names in both languages, this guide uses the Italian version throughout.

Waymarking of Alte Vie 1 and 2 is, on the whole, remarkably thorough. Red and white paint stripes on

rocks, trees, buildings and so on signal the routes themselves, and often bear additional information such as the path number, the next *forcella* or refuge and the time taken to reach it. Alta Via numbers also appear inside a painted triangle.

On clear stretches of trail such as broad tracks, and sometimes on less frequented stretches, waymarks might become less frequent, sometimes just a single paint flash. But in these cases the way ahead is usually unequivocal and junctions are invariably marked. Signposts are also erected at important intersections. Cairns (pyramidal heaps of stones) are also used, and can be life savers in low cloud or misty conditions.

Numerous other numbered footpaths will be encountered too, providing the long-distance and day walker with a marvellous network of routes to choose from.

TERRAIN, MOUNTAIN SAFETY AND WEATHER

Paths are generally well maintained by local authorities together with the combined forces of guides and volunteers from the Italian Alpine Club, although they can be damaged and even washed away by exceptionally heavy winter snowfall or rain. Surfaces are frequently as rugged as will be found on any mountain journey in Europe – a mix of stones, rock and scree, occasionally relieved by rough

Autumn around Rifugio Lavarella (Alta Via 1)

mountain road or forest track, or even the odd woodland path carpeted with soft conifer needles.

Where exposure or steepness exceed normal safe walking limits, artificial protection in the form of metal cable, iron rungs, hoops and ladders is provided; it is not always needed, but it is reassuring in wet or icy conditions and if a large pack is carried.

The main exceptions occur on steep scree just below some passes, and on snow or ice patches in north-facing gullies, especially early in the summer. Great care is needed, and an ice-axe or stock is handy for balance. On such steep terrain a good track is invariably trodden in, but is subject, of course, to freezing and thawing, increasing difficulty.

Walkers should be prepared for substantial vertical ascent and descent and great exposure; nowhere, however, except on the descent of the Schiara on Alta Via 1 (avoidable), is the walker expected to have had rock-climbing experience. Paths are often cunningly constructed in zig-zags, which takes the sting from many a big climb, while some sections resemble scrambles that verge on elementary climbs.

Holiday insurance policies usually cover mountain walking, provided specialist equipment such as ice-axe, rope, and crampons are not used, though it is advisable to check the small print. In any case the E111 form for reciprocal health services is recommended for British and European walkers to cover a visit to the doctor or hospital.

The trail near Passo Giau (Alta Via 1)

Should an accident or illness occur and you need urgent help, use the international distress call: a series of six signals per minute, followed by a minute's pause and then repeated. The reply is three signals per minute, interspersed with a minute's pause. The distress signal can be given in whichever way seems most likely to attract attention: such as blowing a whistle, shouting, or flashing a torch or the sun in a mirror.

Mountain rescue can be initiated from a cell phone, public phone or the nearest refuge – dial 118 and ask for *soccorso alpino* (mountain rescue). Remember that once a rescue is put in motion you are liable for the entire cost of the operation, and if a helicopter is deployed a substantial sum will be incurred, so ensure the decision to summon help is the best or only option. Members of mountaineering and associated clubs are usually covered for such operations.

Of course such an event is highly improbable for walkers who are properly equipped and provisioned, experienced with map and compass, who keep a weather eye open and are fit enough to deal with the day's planned itinerary.

The weather in the Dolomites is generally drier than that in the Alps farther west and north, and there is a tendency towards long, clear spells with calm winds and low average humidity. However periods of rain and low cloud can persist; and even when these clear, afternoon thunderstorms can become a regular and predictable feature. If cumulo-nimbus clouds with great vertical development are observed building during the morning and early afternoon, care should be taken to be clear of peaks, ridges and fixed ironmongery – all prone to lightening strike – by the time the storms break. Often the late evening reverts to fine conditions.

Weather in the south of the region is more subject to the effect of damp winds from the plain rising over the Dolomites' southern slopes and causing greater precipitation: this is particularly pronounced in the Vette Feltrine on Alta Via 2.

Local daily newspapers carry forecasts, though once on an Alta Via, refuges are the most likely source of information; the majority post multilingual weather forecast bulletins daily, as do tourist information offices in the valley towns.

Should you have access to the internet, www.meteoalpin.com covers the Veneto and South Tyrol regions with reports in German, Italian and English, while www.arpa.veneto.it/csvdi/bollettino gives detailed forecasts for the Veneto Dolomites and foothills, but only in Italian at present.

Both of the Alte Vie are feasible from mid-June through to late September, corresponding with refuge opening periods. Note that early season walkers must be prepared to deal with snow-blocked gullies and late visitors with early closures of accommodation (always phone ahead). However, both seasonal extremes mean fewer other users, as well as an improved chance of encountering wildlife.

Temperatures in the Dolomite region can vary widely, depending on altitude and weather conditions. Maximum temperatures are around the mid-20s °C (77°F) June to September, peaking July–August around 30°C (86°F) in the valleys. Minima are about 10°C (50°F), though cool conditions can be accentuated by wind-chill, and it is not unknown for snow flurries to occur. Late August and September are probably the best time to visit the Dolomites in an average year. Late-lying snow has long since melted, and the area often enjoys quiet, clear weather before the nights draw in and the first snows dust the highest peaks late October.

ACCOMMODATION, SUPPLIES AND SERVICES

By far the majority of continental walkers stay overnight in a refuge (*rifugio*) or mountain inn (*albergo*). As will be seen in this guide, refuges vary considerably in size and sophistication. CAI, the Italian Alpine Club, and its Trento branch, SAT, own and runs a good proportion of them, but private enterprise is represented too. They all serve food and drink and will provide a bed for as few as eight people or as many as 130. Some offer catering and facilities of a high standard, others are more basic, and several are accessible by four-wheel drive vehicles or cable-cars. Remote huts are supplied by ingenious mechanised cableways.

In the CAI-operated huts, as a move to cut down on energy and water consumption, bed linen is no longer supplied and it is compulsory for guests to bring their own lightweight sleeping sheet. Blankets are always provided, so a sleeping bag is unnecessary. Sleeping quarters range from a bunk bed (*cuccetta*) in a dormitory (*dormitorio*) to two-bed rooms (*camera a due letti*). Many huts now have a shower (*doccia*), timer operated and activated with a token (*gettone*). Boots and bulky equipment are usually left in the entrance hall, and flip-flops or slippers often provided for guests.

During the high season (late July to late August), advance reservations are necessary especially on weekends. Cancellations must be notified too, so that vacancies may be filled and in order to avoid the needless launch of rescue operations. Nearly all the refuges have a telephone number for bookings, and attempts will be

made to converse in English; an Italian phrase book is, nevertheless, useful. Some walkers turn up with no prior booking: provided you are early, there is some chance you will be accommodated. It's always a good habit to phone ahead just in case a hut is closed due to restoration or adverse weather.

Before setting out purchase a prepaid phone card for using public phones (on sale at tobacconists and newspaper stands – remove the dotted corner before use). Otherwise many refuges have a pay-as-you-use phone system. Remember to include the zero of the area code when dialling, even for local calls. The only exception are calls to cell phones (no zero) and emergency numbers (such as 118).

Members of CAI and the numerous similar organisations from other countries with a reciprocal agreement are eligible for reduced rates at Alpine Club refuges – about 50% for a bed and a 10% discount on food and drinks.

A wide variety of sustaining food is served, such as thick vegetable soup (*minestrone*), omnipresent pasta with an array of sauces starting with the hearty meat *ragù*, eggs and potatoes. The South Tyrol speciality Kaiserschmarm (akin to a crepe with dried fruit and liberally spread with jam) is a popular dessert and a meal in itself. Italian beers are weaker than German types, but the wines make up for it. Coffee comes strong

Tamer/S. Sebastiano group (Alta Via 1)

and black in small cups (*espresso*), with frothy hot milk in ordinary cups (*cappuccino*) or weaker and milky for breakfast (*caffè latte*). Mineral water (*acqua minerale*) is a good idea if the water's not drinkable (*non potabile*).

Collecting individual refuges' rubber stamp impressions, for example in the back of this guide book, is entertaining: a full tally presented to the Tourist Offices in Belluno (for Alta Via 1) or Feltre (for Alta Via 2) will be greeted with congratulatory noises and a commemorative badge.

Money wise, apart from branches in the terminal towns no banks are passed, so adequate cash (in Euros) should be carried. (Cortina d'Ampezzo, off Alta Via 1, and San Martino di Castrozza, off Alta Via 2,

both contain all supplies and services, including ATMs.) The odd refuge will accept credit cards, but these, understandably, are rare as hens' teeth. Prices in Italy generally are notably lower than those in adjacent European countries.

With such a generous scattering of refuges along most of both Alte Vie, it is hardly surprising that campers are in a minority. Lightweight camping is not very popular in the Dolomites and is not allowed in the protected park areas traversed by the Alte Vie.

Moreover, intending campers should be prepared to carry plenty of water. Then, unless the refuges are used for the occasional meal, restocking of basic groceries and hardware usually entails a considerable detour

21

off-route to the nearest town. This can be achieved by using buses (often quite regular) or hitching lifts, but would need to be allowed for in terms of time and cost.

The real advantages of camping, as ever, are its cheapness and the great sense of independence it bestows upon the walker. Freedom from the constraints of crowded accommodation in high season is reward enough for those willing to carry the extra weight. Pitches will often be around the 2000m mark, while official campsites are only found at much lower levels and are therefore unlikely to be used, unless the walking is to be broken into stages by the use of car or bus services.

The final accommodation option consists of the permanent, unsupervised bivouac hut (*bivacco*), sited in high or out-of-the-way places. These are always open and provide shelter free of charge for those on extended climbs or walks. However, only a handful are passed on these Alte Vie. Of metal or more traditional construction (those at lower levels may be a deserted farm building), they are by nature small, rudimentary and only as clean as the previous occupants. Bunks and basic kitchen space will usually be found, but you will need to be self-sufficient in food, fuel and sleeping gear. Just how welcome a bivouac hut is will depend upon the time of day, weather conditions and your state of enthusiasm. In any case, guard against fire, clean up after yourself and remember to close the door when you leave.

Visitors will find Italy a hospitable country, and mountain refuges extend this welcome right up to the high paths used by walkers on Alte Vie 1 and 2.

CLOTHING AND EQUIPMENT

Sound quality equipment is essential in the Dolomites for the summer season. Naturally, experienced walkers have their own ideas on what gear to use but the following notes will help determine its suitability for a trek on an Alta Via.

A comfortable rucksack is top of the list, then versatile clothing to cope with potentially dramatic changes in weather and temperature levels is absolutely essential. Multiple thin layers providing flexible degrees of insulation are preferable to bulky sweaters, duvet jackets and heavy trousers. Shell clothing in the form of cagoule and over-trousers or a waterproof poncho with room for a rucksack is equally necessary as summer storms can be heavy; rain, wind and low air temperatures at altitude present a real threat if not adequately protected against.

With luck, shorts will be required, as will a lightweight shirt and spare clothing for use in refuges or to change into. Several mountain lakes are passed, and the hardier souls may wish to have a swimming costume when the weather smiles.

Below Piz Duleda, looking north (Alta Via 2)

A sun hat, sunglasses and high-factor suncream are all indispensable – remember that the sun's strength is multiplied many times over in the thin air at these altitudes. Most of the Dolomites are formed from pale rock and, depending on the time of year they are visited, may be partly snow-covered on the higher reaches. The dazzling and burning effects of all this reflected ultra-violet radiation can be well imagined.

The ground underfoot is often exceptionally rough, and boots and feet can take quite a hammering. Stout footwear that provides adequate ankle support, cushioning and grip on steep slopes is essential. On easier stretches, ordinary trainers might suffice (and are useful in refuges), but they afford insufficient protection on more serious terrain.

Many walkers now use telescopic poles, a great help when descending steep slopes with a loaded rucksack.

While hut-hoppers will need only a light sheet sleeping bag and towel, for campers a two-season sleeping bag will not be much comfort on its own; however, combined with a bag-liner or thermal underwear and a closed-cell bed mat, it should be warm enough.

A lightweight torch is useful in refuges (where 'lights out' is 10pm–6am). Mountain peaks can obscure the sun long before it has actually set. Spare batteries and bulb should be carried, as shops are few and far between. A headtorch is recommended for exploring the wartime tunnels, such as Lagazuoi on AV1. Italy adopts daylight savings time from April until late October.

23

Camping Gaz fuel for cooking in the familiar blue cartridges is widely available in Italy. Water, on the other hand, is not universally abundant in these steep, rocky mountains, and backpackers should be prepared on occasions to carry an abundant supply. Some stretches of trail are, in fact, completely dry. Having said that, streams and meltwater are encountered, and liquid refreshment of all kinds can be obtained from refuges. Water containers – at least 1 litre per person per day – are clearly important, and purifying tablets will provide peace of mind where the source of water is suspect.

A comprehensive first-aid kit is a wise precaution against injury or accident. A snake-bite kit is also rec-ommended, though the risk of needing to use it is small unless extensive exploration off the track is planned. The viper (*vipera*), light grey and modest in size with diamond patterns on its back, is the only poisonous snake here, and currently the most effective treatment device is the battery-operated Ecobite (available from Ecobrands, UK). It delivers a series of mini electric shocks that decompose the venom and alleviate discomfort.

Stout plastic bags are invaluable for keeping rucksack contents dry in rainy weather and for separating clothing, food, documents and so on. A map case and compass are useful too, as is a small Italian dictionary or phrase-book.

Note: while there are many

Rifugio Coldai looks across to the mighty Pelmo on Alta Via 1

essentials to be carried, take care not to overload your pack. Be honest with yourself, and leave anything not strictly necessary either at home or in your car. The walking itself is hard enough, and will certainly not be enhanced by a painful back. Remember this is supposed to be a holiday!

If the traverse of Forcella della Marmolada on Alta Via 2 is anticipated, involving the ascent of a small glacier, it is advisable to take crampons, ice-axe and rope. Moreover the concluding stage of Alta Via 1 entails a *via ferrata* (see following notes), though this can be easily detoured. Otherwise, it is possible to complete either Alta Via covered by this guide without equipment additional to normal mountain-walking gear. However, while both routes are for walkers, it is necessary to add that gradients and exposure are steep in places. Early in the season, up to about mid-July, an ice-axe and even crampons are a useful safeguard on late-lying snow on some of the higher north-facing cols.

Via ferrata notes: in addition to the Schiara route in the final stage of AV1, a number of aided climbs can be followed by experienced climbers as variants from the Alte Vie. A suitable protection kit can be obtained from outdoor shops in the Dolomites region. Essentials include a helmet, full harness, two large gate karabiners to allow clipping onto cables and rungs with large diameters and a 4m length of 11mm rope (see photo).

Via ferrata kit

It will be readily appreciated that by taking along this simple protection kit, scope for off-route exploration on aided paths, rock outcrops and *vie ferrate* is greatly enhanced for those with a head for heights and used to mountain scrambling or rock climbing. The Dolomite peaks and walls are peppered with *vie ferrate*, steep and often exposed rock routes which rely extensively on metal cables, rungs and ladders. For more information see Cicerone's guides to *via ferratas* in the Dolomites.

25

GEOLOGY, FLORA AND FAUNA

The Dolomites lie on a base of crystalline schist. Various deposits, including sandstone, loam and chalk, were subsequently laid down over this. During early geological periods, the whole region was submerged beneath a coral sea, much like those that exist today. Coral reefs and other accumulations of marine organisms eventually formed the massive limestone structures with no obvious stratification which are particularly prevalent in the western Dolomites: the Putia, Odle, Sella and Pale groups and even more compact mountains like the Marmolada.

In later periods (Jurassic and Cretaceous), many friable forms of grey limestone, pink ammonite limestone and loam were laid down, found mainly in the Puez and Vette Feltrine groups.

Following the formation of these great marine deposits and their partial transformation into dolomite rock, the seabed began to rise as titanic forces shifted and convulsed the earth's crust. In some places the rock strata broke up, in others becoming folded and overlapped, reversing the original positions of the layers. Over the millions of years it takes for geological changes to occur, upheaval following upheaval, the existing conformation of the Dolomites was reached.

By contrast, the effect of glaciation and erosion by frost, rain and wind are relatively fast-moving. Progressive landslides and the inexorable flaking of rock walls are clear for the walker on either Alta Via to see: in places, the routes have been redirected round landslips and associated debris.

The story of living organisms that populated these sedimentary and cretaceous rocks, before they were elevated into mountain form, is told in myriad fossil remains. These imprints of creatures and plants, shells and corals, not to mention dinosaurs, are spread through various layers, and the observant traveller will spot many examples – particularly on the limestone tablelands of Puez and Pale di San Martino.

Perhaps more than any other Alpine region, the Dolomites are richly abundant in flora, starting with

Globeflowers backed by Ra Gusela

olive trees on the northern fringes of the Veneto plain. Between valley bottoms and the bare, rocky heights exists a profusion of trees, bushes and undergrowth, with species too numerous to catalogue here; among them are found rhododendrons, whortleberries, hazelnuts, wild cherries and raspberries, juniper and ferns. Wild flowers add brilliant colour to meadow, alp and high path alike, with July the premier month. Included are such protected species as the Rhaetian poppy, purple saxifrage, spotted gentian, devil's claw, pink cinquefoil, edelweiss and divine lilies and orchids. It is always with a sense of wonder and incredulity that you come across brightly coloured species thriving in cracks and crannies above 2500m. Amongst these true alpines, the jewels of high mountain locations, are the brilliant blue stars of the spring gentian, the delicate purple alpine pansy and the bright pink flower-cushions of rock jasmine. Thankfully the practice of picking wild flowers is dropping off as visitors learn respect for this vulnerable environment. With so many visitors using the mountains for sporting and leisure activities, conservation of natural habitats should be uppermost in everyone's mind.

In terms of wildlife, commonest by far is the marmot, a cuddly, beaver-like animal up to 60cms (2ft) in length which hibernates from late October to mid-April. Although world-wide there are some 13 species, it is found

Fat gentian trumpets

Dolomite endemic Campanula morettiana

27

Delicate Rhaetian poppies

Alpine snowbells are amongst the earliest blooms

in its original habitat only in the Alps and High Tatras, its wolf-whistle warning cry heard on grassy and stony slopes up to about 2700m. Marmots live gregariously in burrows reaching down 3m and extending as much as 10m in length, with several exits. Each individual weighs about 5 or 6kg, living off plant greenery and, during hibernation, body fat. In late May or early June, females give birth to up to six naked and blind young.

Another exciting high-mountain mammal to observe is the wild mountain goat or chamois, though shyness makes it more elusive. These animals can sometimes be spotted in herds on precipitous rocky slopes, over which they move with uncanny agility, living in groups of between 15 and 30 individuals. Their light fawn colouring and short hooked horns easily distinguish them from the hefty ibex, which sport impressive long grooved horns, used effectively by young males in mock battles. Re-introduced 30 years ago after being hunted to extinction in the 17th century, healthy groups are easily observed around the Croda

del Becco at the start of AV1 and the valleys south of the Marmolada on AV2.

Other creatures which may, with good fortune and patience, be glimpsed in the forests include stags and roe deer and squirrels. On the high rock plateaux, alpine hares and even ermine might be seen. Adders (or vipers) are common today in much of the Alps, so care should be taken to avoid being bitten if one is encountered at close quarters (see 'Clothing and Equipment').

A further potential danger from wildlife concerns ticks (*zecche*) in the Feltre and Belluno districts, namely the final stages of both Alte Vie. Some carry Lyme's disease and even TBE (tick-borne encephalitis), which can be life-threatening for humans. After traversing heavily wooded zones with thick undergrowth, check for any suspect black pinpoint spots or unusual itching. Ticks require careful removal: they firstly need suffocating – up to 5 minutes smothered in a cream such as toothpaste – then you should grasp the head with tweezers and pull out carefully. If in doubt go to the nearest hospital, where an antibiotic may be prescribed as a precaution.

Bird species are represented by the occasional golden eagle, white partridge, imperial raven, jackdaw, alpine chaffinch and the cumbersome capercaillie, a wood-grouse once much prized as a game bird. Despite the Italian penchant for hunting that has decimated birds of prey along with many forest-dwelling creatures, it is encouraging to note the ongoing establishment of nature parks in which wildlife is now protected: the Puez-Odle and Paneveggio/Pale di San Martino parks on Alta Via 2 are good examples, as are the Fanes-Sennes-Braies and Dolomiti d'Ampezzo parks on Alta Via 1. The exten-sive Dolomiti Bellunesi National Park covers the final stages of both.

PHOTOGRAPHY

Passing so much unusual topography on both Alte Vie, the prospects for photography are exceptionally inter-esting. Surpassing all else, however, is the quality of light, especially in fine weather. Sunrise and sunset are the two most magical moments of the day, when the upper crags and sum-mits are lit yellow, golden and deep red by the low sun – unforgettable. At other times, there is a dazzling bril-liance of sunshine on rock and snow, while at lower altitudes farmsteads, barns and settlements add human interest. Even in changeable weather,

The distant peaks of Alta Via 1 from near Rifugio Genova on Alta Via 2

San Martino di Castrozza from Cima della Rosetta (Alta Via 2)

rain and mist invariably give way to dramatic clearances.

A perfect 'compromise' camera is a lightweight 35mm compact with a good inbuilt zoom and padded pouch, small enough for a shirt or rucksack pocket, and easy to operate on awkward sections of path.

It is advisable to take film stock with you, although it can be purchased en route – at inflated prices. Heat is film's number one enemy and can significantly degrade the quality of the processed image, particularly colour. Unused and exposed film stock can be packed deep within your pack, surrounded by insulating items like spare clothing and sleeping bag.

HOW TO USE THIS GUIDE

In order to split both routes into manageable chunks, Alta Via 1 appears in three sections, Alta Via 2 in four. Each section represents approximately three days of walking, taking into account stops for meals, photography, off-route detours and occasional bad weather. Each section also starts and ends at a town or major road pass, giving scope for breaking the walk to obtain supplies or to be picked up by car.

The principal official variants are outlined in the text in blue paragraphs and appear on the sketch-maps too, facilitating a choice of alternative routings should circumstances dictate. The stages in this guide, how-

The Averau, part of the magnificent panorama from Nuvolau

ever, are suggestions only, and individual walkers may well develop different objectives to suit their own pace and available time.

Important landmarks along the trail, such as refuges, saddles or cols, road passes and path junctions are printed in bold type and are preceded by the time it takes to reach them from the previous landmark. (Timings are based on a moderately laden walker's steady pace and do not include stops.) In line with European usage, heights above sea level, in brackets, are expressed in metres (1000m = 3279ft).

The locations, owners, capacities, opening periods, accessibility and telephone numbers of refuges along the way are included, as are occasional references to possible camping pitches and car parking space near the path. Readers will find sectional profiles accompanying each stage of the walks, showing the ascent/descent involved, alongside timing.

Route directions throughout are given for the south-bound walker and are abbreviated in the text: R = right, L = left. Compass points are also expressed as initial letters, eg NE = north-east, S = south. Alta Via 1 and 2 appear as AV1 and AV2.

A comprehensive glossary has been included, giving translations of Italian words the mountain walker is likely to find useful.

Changes to Alta Via routings and their variants do occur from time to time, as do the specifications of refuges. However, to the best of the authors' knowledge, all the information contained in this guide is accurate at the time of going to press.

ALTA VIA 1

STAGE 1:
LAGO DI BRAIES TO RIFUGIO LAGAZUOI

From lovely Lago di Braies, Alta Via 1 ascends through forest and a rocky valley to its first pass under the peak of Croda del Becco, with outstanding views ahead. On good tracks past patches of forest, lakes and mountain farmsteads, and taking in several refuges, height is gradually gained as the route penetrates higher mountain terrain. A steep *forcella* is crossed to another lake, and you approach a rugged area of cliffs and rock towers rich in relics from the conflict between Italian and Austrian troops in World War I. At 2752m, Rifugio Lagazuoi is the highest point reached so far, perched at the top of a cable-car line from Passo Falzarego and providing sensational panoramas over this region of the Dolomites.

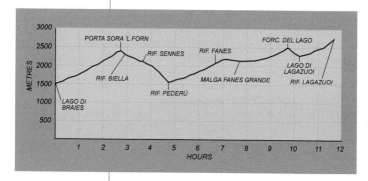

The official start of AV1 is the beautiful lake known as Lago di Braies in the picturesque Valle di Braies. The lower valley itself contains only the odd shop, other buildings being dwellings, restaurants and hotels, so provisions for the first part of the walk need to be carried in,

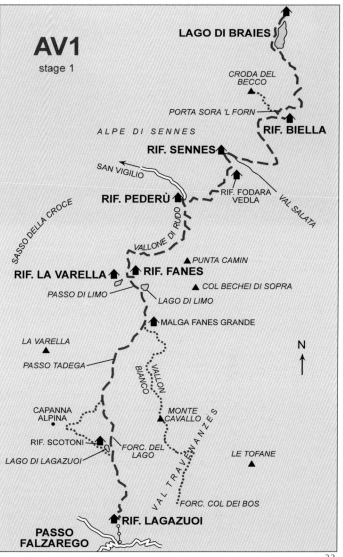

Lago di Braies backed by towering Croda del Becco

particularly if you are backpacking. There are good shops at Monguelfo and Villabassa in Val Pusteria.

At first the valley approaches are dominated by rock spire of Sasso del Signore (2447m) and its buttresses to the E, but before long the southern horizon is filled by the great north face of Croda del Becco soaring above pine forest to 2810m.

LAGO DI BRAIES (1494m) – *a very popular holiday and weekend family destination, and justly so. Its turquoise waters are fringed with little white shingle beaches and encircled by a good, much-walked track. Not surprisingly, there is ample car parking (fee-paying), boating on the lake, souvenir shops, a bar/restaurant and a marvellous alpine-style Grand Hotel famous for hosting the Beatles' personal guru, Maharishi Mahesh Yogi, in the 1960s (Hotel Lago di Braies tel. 0474-748602 open May to Oct, special rates for walkers). Camping, however, is forbidden – understandably considering the location's natural qualities and the heavy use it receives. The area comes under the Parco Naturale Fanes-Sennes-Braies. Several buses a day run up to here from the railway station at Villabassa (late June to Sept).*

At the rear of the hotel, take the clearly signed broad track (1) past a chapel, undulating pleasantly along the lake's west shore through pine forest. At the S end, leave the shoreline path at a prominent signpost and climb through low conifers in steady zigzags to a junction at the top of a modest ravine. Keep R, continuing the steep winding ascent in forest with the occasional marvellous views to glaciated peaks in the distant Tyrol. After a short rocky passage equipped with steel cable (the first of several aided sections, but here quite superfluous except in wet or icy conditions) another junction is encountered above the tree line. Bear W (R), following waymarks on rocks. On a level at first (possible wild camping if water carried), the route enters a closed upper valley known as Forno (or 'furnace') for its heat-trapping capacity, which will quickly become clear to midsummer walkers. Over scree and boulders beneath the high, striated cliffs of Monte Muro L, head up this rocky valley to emerge at

Lovely view of Lago di Braies from the path to Rifugio Biella

• **Side trip:** from the crucifix at the pass, an entertaining path zigzags cleverly NW up a steep exposed corner of mountain to the summit of Croda del Becco (2810m), haunt of proud ibex: the panorama from this elevated spot is quite breathtaking. 2hrs return time.

2 hrs 45 min – **PORTA SORA 'L FORN** (2388m) – *The view in clear weather is immense and amply rewards the relentless climb from Lago di Braies. To the SW glitters the Marmolada's glacier, in the S rises the wedge of M. Pelmo, to the SE lies Monte Cristallo – profiles which will become familiar companions on the journey S.•*

Below to the L stands

10 min – **RIFUGIO BIELLA** (2300m) – *tel.0436-866991, CAI, 45 places, open 20 June to end Sept. Welcoming, well-run hut with the bare essentials.*

AV1 now follows the jeep track (path 6) W then SE round a large depression in the Alpe di Sennes, turning sharply W

Walkers at Porta Sora'l Forn

round Col di Siores and dropping to join a track from Val Salata *(possible exit via Rif. Ra Stua to the Cortina-Dobbiaco road and buses)*, before reaching the pleasantly situated

45 min – **RIFUGIO SENNES** (2116m) – *tel. 0474-*

501092, privately owned, 63 places, open mid-June to end Sept. Hot showers and hearty meals.

Leave the refuge with its diminutive lake, SE on path 7, still on the jeep track, once an old military road. The way crosses the flowery Pian di Lasta, ignoring a L turn to modern Rifugio Fodara Vedla (*tel. 0474-501093 private,*

Stunning views from the first col above the Biella hut, including Monte Pelmo in the distance

• Though this area belongs to the Parco Naturale Fanes-Sennes-Braies, a private jeep will take up to six passengers at a time – at a steep price – from Rifugio Pederù to Rifugio Fanes or La Varella, much to the disdain of walkers whom it passes and covers in dust!

•• High peaks punctuate the edges of this broad pasture amphitheatre run through with streams and featuring a curious series of limestone slab terracing dotted with pine trees: above Rifugio La Varella and tiny Lago Verde rises the gently sloping Sasso della Croce formation culminating in Sasso delle Dieci and Sasso delle Nove; to the SW, Cima Paron and La Varella; to the E, Col Bechei di Sopra and to the NE Punta Camin.

sleeps 47, open June–Oct) and zigzags down between Colle della Macchina to the N and Colle di Rù to the S. Descending more steeply, the track, now in patchy forest, reaches a gully and arrives at

1 hr – **RIFUGIO PEDERÙ** (1548m) – *tel. 0474-501086, privately owned guesthouse, 30 places, open early June to end Sept. Connected NW to San Vigilio di Marebbe in Val Badia (① 0474-501037) by a motorable road and regular bus service.•*

A rough mountain road now climbs S up Vallone di Rudo with numerous hairpins and path short cuts, and passes Lago Piciodil in its wild rocky environment to reach trees and a pasture basin with

2 hrs – **RIFUGIO FANES** (2060m) – *tel. 0474-501097, privately owned, 80 places, open beg. June to end Oct. The building is decorated with wartime relics, including large shell cases on the balcony.*

    As the atmosphere in this rambling establishment can verge on boisterous, a quieter option W, 10 min off the main route, is Rifugio La Varella tel. 0474-501079, privately owned, 50 places, open mid-June to mid October.••

Climbing SE, the rough track (n.11) soon reaches Passo di Limo (2172m) and the popular day-trip destination of Lago di Limo, thereafter dropping S to the dairy farm

1 hr – **MALGA FANES GRANDE** (2102m) – *tel. mobile 347/8782776, privately owned, sleeps 12, open mid-summer (sleeping bag needed).* The track proceeds across a marshy depression.

Variant to Val Travenanzes: The L fork, path 17, heads SE then S up Vallon Bianco via Bivacco 'Della Pace' (*12 places, no water*) to the summit of Monte Castello and along the crest to Monte Cavallo (2912m). The ridge was intensively fortified by the Austrians during World War I

On the trail near Malga Fanes Grande

and still bears the remains of timbered trenches, tunnels and artificial pathways clinging precariously to the shattered rock. Despite these attractions, the ascent is rough and the descent into Val Travenanzes dangerously steep. It comes out at abandoned Malga Travenanzes before a climb to rejoin the main route near Forcella Col dei Bos, meaning that Rifugio Lagazuoi is cut out. Allow 6–7 hrs, and remember, it is not an easy traverse.

AV1 (path 11) keeps to the mule track, ascending gently to Passo Tadega (2153m), past a branch R for the summits of La Varella (3055m) and Cunturines (3064m). Ahead, over clumps of trees, rears the wedge-shaped Cima del Lago, with the next destination Forcella del Lago visible to its L. A short distance on, fork L at a signed junction (2117m). •

A steady climb concludes with a steeper section to reach the conspicuous notch of impressive

2 hrs – **FORCELLA DEL LAGO** (2486m).

A rough scree path drops quickly due S to join a well

• **Note:** the descent from the ensuing *forcella* entails a particularly steep descent over loose scree and rock, best attempted by those with a steady head for heights who can move securely on difficult ground. It is easily avoided by taking the straightforward variant below which rejoins the main route at Lago di Lagazuoi.

39

The final climb to Rifugio Lagazuoi

defined and waymarked track (n.20) above the attractive green expanse of Lago di Lagazuoi (2182m).

Variant via Rifugio Scotoni: A longer but easier alternative to the Forcella del Lago lies in taking the R path fork at the 2117m path junction and over Col Locia (2069m) around the NW corner of Cima del Lago. This path (11) drops W (ignore a path climbing S) through patchy forest to a jeep track above Capanna Alpina (1726m, useful exit for bus to San Cassiano in Val Badia or Passo Falzarego). Just before the building is reached, turn sharp L (SE) up Vallone di Lagazuoi on track 20, past Rifugio Scotoni (1985m, *tel. 0471-847330, privately owned, 19 places, open late June to end Sept*) to meet the main route at Lago di Lagazuoi. Allow an extra hour for the detour.

From the lake, taking the R fork, climb gradually almost due S across the Alpe di Lagazuoi over undulating rocky terrain, with the awesome line of cliffs on Lagazuoi Grande ahead L.

At a prominent signpost, AV1 makes a bee-line for the refuge, visible (in clear conditions) on the ridge ahead. Shaley slopes have been bulldozed for winter skiers and the 200m climb is an uninspiring trudge, usually a snow crossing until midsummer. Once again, however, and this is so often the case in the Dolomites, effort is rewarded.

2 hrs – **RIFUGIO LAGAZUOI** (2752m) – *tel. 0436-867303, privately owned, 75 places, open 20 June to 10*

Rifugio Lagazuoi is a marvellous lookout

Oct. Accommodation is in both modern dormitories and private rooms, with hot showers and restaurant-quality meals at hand.

This is the highest point reached so far and, given good weather, the views are unforgettable, with range upon range of mountains laid out like a map in all directions. There is also a cable-car ride down to Passo Falzarego for more of the same, with the added bonus, if required, of public transport right down to the fleshpots of Cortina d'Ampezzo (① 0436-3231, all supplies and services). However, the descent is a long one and steps must be retraced.

World War I trenches on Lagazuoi

The refuge may be bypassed if time or weather press, or if its attractions aren't sufficient to justify the climb up… In this case, before the final 200m climb, keep L above a marshy depression and head SE to Forcella Lagazuoi (2571m).

STAGE 2:
RIFUGIO LAGAZUOI TO PASSO DURAN

From World War I galleries hewn into the Lagazuoi and Castelletto mountains, close to the great summits of Le Tofane above the bustling resort of Cortina d'Ampezzo, Alta Via 1 climbs to the Nuvolau. This rocky peak with its popular refuge is one of the finest panoramic viewpoints in the entire Dolomite range. A steep descent leads to grassier hillsides and a succession of passes in easy, mixed terrain beneath the imposing bulk of Monte Pelmo; this giant is subsequently traversed via a dramatic northern *forcella*, and its southern flanks circled. Rough mountain roads lead to a high farm and the ascent to Rifugio Coldai, a good base for experienced climbers keen to reach the summit of Monte Civetta. In sensational mountain scenery under the Civetta's 7km-long west face, you leave the delightful Lago Coldai, drop down flowery Val Civetta and cross lower cols, in and out of forest. Three more refuges are passed in much wilder and quieter surrounds before the trail arrives at pastureland around Passo Duran.

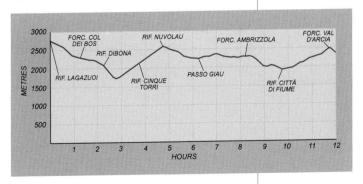

Caves and scattered timbers on the slopes of all the surrounding mountains date from World War I, when this

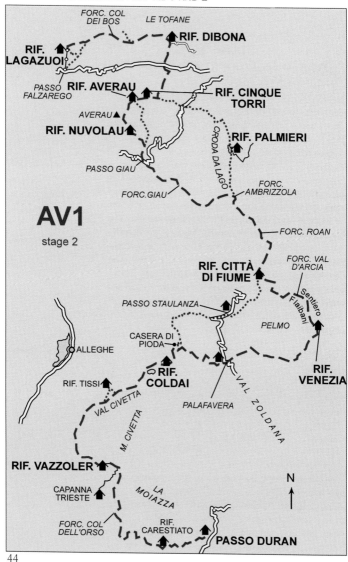

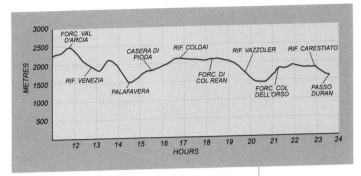

area was given over to fighting between Austrian and Italian troops. Old fortifications abound. In fact, the crest of Piccolo Lagazuoi, beneath the refuge, contains a labyrinth of underground wartime passages. During the 1915–18 conflict, the main summit was held by the Austrians whose attempt to dislodge the Italians from the Cengia Martini ledge half way down the south wall, using powerful mines, produced scars on the mountainside which are clearly visible today.

In turn, the Italians excavated a remarkable and very steep 1100m-long tunnel (Galleria Lagazuoi) through the heart of the mountain itself, entailing a climb of 230m. This has been 'renovated' for sure-footed intrepid visitors to explore, and is an unforgettable experience. Slippery, dark and claustrophobic describe it, as does exhilarating! A torch is essential, preferably a head-lamp, though hand-held flares can be purchased at the refuge.

Galleria Lagazuoi variant: A path (marked 'G') leads down behind the cable-car station bearing L via trenches to the actual tunnel entrance. A good 45 min are needed for the knee-jarring descent via steps and ladders, accompanied by a reassuring hand-cable. Finally emerging in daylight at the Cengia Martini, you turn L for several narrow rock passages before dropping to the foot of the cliff to join a steep path. To return uphill and rejoin the AV1, go L on path n.402 climbing to Forcella Lagazuoi or Travenanzes

The Castelletto outcrop

(a good 30 minutes). Otherwise continue down to Passo Falzarego and take the cable-car back up to the refuge. Allow 1 hr 30 min in descent as far as the road pass.

From Rifugio Lagazuoi, AV1 goes back down the snow-bound slope and R (NE) on path 401 for Forcella Lagazuoi, then the clear path traversing E beneath avalanche barriers to Forcella Travenanzes (2507m) – not the obvious path dropping R directly to Passo Falzarego. The maze of trods and tracks in the vicinity bears witness to its popularity, but keep ahead NE (wild pitches near streams) and turn R at a waymarked boulder, on path 402.

Val Travenanzes stretches away to the L, an immensely rugged place, littered with boulders and shattered rock and bounded to the W by the screes and rock towers of Lagazuoi Grande, to the E by the Tofane massif.

Near the path stands a World War I memorial stone, surrounded by rusty barbed-wire, shell cases and old boot soles – startlingly graphic reminders of the bitter fighting which took place here 85 or so years ago. A little further on are the remains of buildings and slit trenches. Walking S, you soon reach

1 hr 15 min – **FORCELLA COL DEI BOS** (2290m) and promising views S to the Cinque Torri and Nuvolau, on the route ahead.

AV1 now turns L (E) on path 404 for a beautiful stretch cutting the base of the overpowering Tofana di Rozes. A fork is quickly reached for the climb for the entrance of the Galleria del Castelletto.

Castelletto variant: The Castelletto, a SW spur of the Tofane, was held by the Austrians and dominated Italian positions at Col dei Bos and in Val Costeana. As a result, it was the subject of repeated and bloody direct attacks until finally, at 3.30pm on July 11th 1916, the summit was blown up by 35 tons of explosive, causing terrible loss of life amongst the defenders. A further day of hard fighting ensued before Italian Alpine troops were able to claim the shattered summit.

The gallery, suitably repaired for visits, is a moving testimony to those terrible events. A torch will be needed, and a steady head in places.

Take the narrow path up to the base of the rock, then climb the small cliff (metal rungs and cables) to gain access to the cave entrance. The gallery itself zigzags up inside

First World War tunnel entrance on the Castelletto

the mountain, about 6m from the cliff face. Wooden steps and handholds are provided where the gradient steepens. Hollows hewn into walls at intervals formed sleeping quarters, ammunition stores, gun chambers and latrines; deep grooves in the rock floor were worn in by the movement of artillery. Information boards explain features within the gallery before the route passes the explosion crater and emerges at the cliff face near the top of the Castelletto (2675m). Allow about an hour from the turn-off after Forcella Col dei Bos. (Here starts the difficult *Via Ferrata Lipella* – for equipped experts only – to Tre Dita and optional 3225m Tofana di Rozes summit, then path descent via Rifugio Giussani to Rifugio Dibona.)

The main route continues E, with superb views E to the Sorapiss over Cortina and Antelao SE. A junction marks the descent (path 442) via a cableway loading point and jeep track leading to

1 hr – **RIFUGIO DIBONA** (2083m) – *tel. 0436-860294, privately owned, 70 places, open 20 June to 20 Sept.*

Follow the dirt track downhill to the first curve where you go off R for knee-jarring path 442 through wood to cross the Cortina-Passo Falzarego road at Cianzopè (1724m). •
    Continuing S, a narrow motorable road is followed briefly before 439 breaks off into wood to cut corners. You quickly reach the realm of rock climbers at the Cinque Torri rock formations which overshadow family-run

• To save 300m in ascent, an effort-free ride to Rif. Scoiattoli is possible from here by following the road 2km uphill – bus feasible – then the chair lift.

1 hr 30 min – **RIFUGIO CINQUE TORRI** (2137m) – *tel. 0436-2902, privately run, 20 places, open mid-June to end Sept.*
    The extraordinary cluster of five rock towers are all that remain of an ancient turreted mountain. With routes of all grades on their flanks, there is every likelihood of seeing climbers perched high above.
    Not far uphill is another splendidly placed modern

The Cinque Torri backed by the Tofane

establishment, Rifugio Scoiattoli (2225m), named after a famous group of climbers, the 'Squirrels' – tel. 0436-867939, privately run, 25 places, open start July to 20 Sept.

Here, on a grassy alp, the main route and a good variant diverge, re-uniting at Forcella Ambrizzola, 4 hrs distant. The variant is described below when the main route reaches the *forcella*.•

From the path junction near Rifugio Scoiattoli, AV1 climbs steadily S over rocky slopes passing *Rifugio Averau (tel. 0436-4660, private, 21 places, open beg. June to end Sept)* following well-marked and popular path 439 up to

1 hr – RIFUGIO NUVOLAU (2575m) – *tel. 0436-867938, CAI, 25 places, open 25 June to 25 Sept. The rather spartan conditions and understandable water shortage are easily compensated for by the magnificent setting and warm reception.*

The Nuvolau is one of the premier viewpoints in the entire Dolomites region, and in clear conditions panoramas from the rocky crest are of a very special order. Behind to the N lie the Tofane, Lagazuoi and the now dwarfed Cinque Torri,

• An additional alternative as far as Passo Giau is feasible in 1 hr 15 min for those wishing to detour the Nuvolau and avoid the exposed ridge and aided gully. Pretty path 443 due S involves a series of rather abrupt climbs and drops along the E flank of Nuvolau, with good chances of chamois and marmot sightings.

Climbing the ridge to Nuvolau, with Croda da Lago behind

while to the S minor rock towers and ridges lead the eye to the great wedge of Monte Pelmo.

Proceed SE past the flagpole to the end of the little summit ridge to descend a scrambly rock pitch, surprisingly abrupt but fitted with a metal ladder. An easy, flatter section ends at a marker pole on a cliff edge at the rear of the Ra Gusela rock formation, whence a short aided ledge, followed by cable and another ladder. A diagonal route S drops to the grassy meadows around the road pass

1 hr 30 min – **PASSO GIAU** (2236m) – *no bus services. Rifugio Passo Giau tel. 0437-720130, privately owned, 36 places, open beg. June to end Sept. Hotel-grade accommodation.*

Take path 436 to the L of a small chapel, contouring round grassy slopes with wonderful retrospective views to the Nuvolau refuge, the Tofane and, in the W, the Marmolada and Sella group. At the little Forcella di Zònia, bear R beneath Col Piombin to reach a well-defined but unnamed *forcella* (2239m).

AV1 then drops round E in Val Cernera, dominated ahead by the flat-topped bulk of Monte Formin (2657m), before climbing a small valley to cross

1 hr – **FORCELLA GIAU** (2360m). *Marvellous outlook dominated by the majestic bastions of M. Pelmo SE.*

Taking the L (E) path fork and dropping across undulating pasture, AV1 follows Monte Formin's impressive S cliffs and crosses several stream beds before rising to join several other paths converging on

1 hr – **FORCELLA AMBRIZZOLA** (2277m).

Variant from Rifugio Cinque Torri: A mule track is followed E to a fork where you take wide path 437, descending into forest to cross the Cortina-Passo Giau road at Ponte di Rocurto (1708m) then the pretty Rio Costeana stream. The path climbs gently, shaded by conifers, past a turn-off for Val Formin, then, as 434 ascends more steeply NE, turning the sharp northern spur of Croda da Lago. A superb lookout point over the Cortina valley is soon reached, whereafter the variant veers sharply S and coasts easily to beautiful Lago di Federa and delightful family-run

Sunset on Ra Gusela from Passo Giau

2 hrs – **RIFUGIO CRODA DA LAGO 'G. PALMIERI'** (2055m) – *tel. 0436-862085, CAI, 45 places, open mid-June to end Sept. Jeep taxi service to Zuel, S of Cortina.*

Croda da Lago (2701m) rises precipitously to the W, a classic Dolomite mountain with several campaniles – sharp spires of rock – and testing rock-climbing routes.

Take broad path 434 due S climbing flowered scree flanks to Forcella Ambrizzola and rejoining the main route in 45 min.

Rifugio Palmieri at the foot of Croda da Lago

Across chaotic screes and boulders below shapely Becco di Mezzodì (2603m), path 458 leads on SE to Forcella Col Duro (2293m), before dropping gently to pasture and Malga Prendera (2148m) under the great S cliffs of La Rochetta (2496m). With superb views of the Civetta ahead keep R and down for

1 hr – **FORCELLA ROAN** (1996m).

Wooded slopes and grassy terraces beneath Punta Puina on broad path 467 accompany you to Forcella della

Puina (2034m) and a gentle descent over pasture to the track-end in the midst of grazing dairy herds at

30 min – **RIFUGIO CITTÀ DI FIUME** (1918m) – *tel. 0437-720268, CAI, 25 places, open 20 June to 20 Sept. Possible wild pitches in the area – if you can avoid the cows!•*

The ensuing stretch climbs into the wild, snowbound Val d'Arcia for the steep and often tricky traverse on Sentiero Flaibani to Rifugio Venezia and an unforgettable circuit of the Pelmo. A simpler variant is described (below) where the two routes join up at Casera di Pioda.

Leave Rif. Città di Fiume on broad path 480 in gentle ascent E through wood for Forcella Forada and a cru-

Steep scree leading to Forcella Val d'Arcia on the Pelmo

• In the vicinity of the refuge there is a marvellous view between pine trees of **Monte Pelmo**'s imposing N face – an immense wall of screes and rock rising 1000m to 3168m. The Pelmo is one of the great peaks of the Dolomites, massive and commanding from all angles. Its huge southern recess, like some gargantuan armchair, is know as the Caregòn and distinguishes it from afar. As long ago as 800 BC, valley-dwelling huntsmen are believed to have reached the summit, though the first recorded ascent in recent times was made by that British pioneer John Ball in 1857. The normal summit route is not particularly difficult, but it is a long and tiring climb. Enquire of the alpine guide at Rif. Venezia.

cifix (1977m). Turn sharp R in gradual descent to the opening of a rubble-choked gully. Watch carefully for paint splashes on a boulder for the turn L (SE). The steep climb negotiates several hands-on stretches and unstable terrain, eventually emerging on a surprisingly grassy crest and easy terrain below Cima Forada. The path soon gains the awe-inspiring Val D'Arcia and veers L (NE). Across rough, rocky terrain sticking to the left flank of the valley, it rises high above snowfields, to round the valley head and clamber tiringly up mobile scree and snow patches (extra care needed) to join a direct route from Passo Staulanza at

2 hrs – **FORCELLA VAL D'ARCIA** (2476m) *and vast views E over the heavily wooded Boite valley, overshadowed by the pale towering Antelao and the Marmarole.*

The path plunges straight down the loose scree, of no great difficulty if you dig your heels in. Bearing R (ESE) below the Crode di Forca Rossa, it hugs the cliffside with several cable-aided sections before rounding a corner and minor saddle and pointing decidedly R (S). With the refuge in view, the path improves dramatically and a multitude of wild flowers brighten the slopes. Skirting beneath the Pelmo's prominent Spalla Est (eastern shoulder), you drop to

1 hr – **RIFUGIO VENEZIA** (1947m) – *tel. 0436-9684, CAI, 60 places, open mid-June to end Sept. Marvellous hearty soups and sunsets on the Marmarole and Antelao opposite.*

After nearby Passo di Rutorto (1931m), AV1 heads decidedly SW as path 472 dropping across a rocky basin at the foot of soaring walls. A climb through light wood to a marshy saddle sees the route bear W, mostly on a level, immersed in dwarf mountain pines to the signed turn-off at Col delle Crepe (1885m). •

Turn L (NW then SW) following Rio Bianco and path 474 down through forest to the road at

• From here a recommended detour to see fossilised **dinosaur footprints** means continuing on path 472 to the nearby fork R for the 'orme', at the base of the Pelmetto. A faint path rises to a slippery clamber and a prominent fallen rock slab at 2050m, bedecked with over 100 prints dating back 220 million years, when the area was covered by shallow tropical waters. Allow 45 min for the round trip.

1 hr 45 min – **PALAFAVERA** (1507m) – *summer bus service, groceries, campsite and two privately-run refuges: Rifugio Palafavera tel. 0437-789133, 25 places, open 15 June to 20 Sept; Rifugio Monte Pelmo tel. 0437-78935, 8 places, open mid-June to end Sept.*

A chair lift can be used on the next section in lieu of the rather uninteresting motorable farm road W up through patchy forest and undergrowth; its dog-legs can be short-cut at first, though it must eventually be walked up to

1 hr – **CASERA DI PIODA** aka Malga Pioda *(1816m) – drinking water and dairy products available. Good (if rough) car parking.*

Variant from Rif. Città di Fiume: Leave the refuge S across the stream on path 472, dropping through forest to cross a rugged torrent bed, directly under the Pelmo's snowfields and vast Val d'Arcia. After a short descent, AV1 reaches the road pass

1 hr 30min – **PASSO STAULANZA** (1766m) – *and pleasant privately owned Rif. Passo Staulanza tel. 0437-788566, 30 places, open 10 June to end Sept. Bus via Val Zoldana (① 0437-789145, all supplies and services, hotels) to Longarone and trains.*

The following section linking with the Monte Civetta massif leaves much to be desired. Starting on tarmac, it transfers to a rough track, followed by bare mountainside denuded and remodelled for the demands of winter skiing.

Follow the road down SW from Forcella Staulanza for about 1km, turning off R at the first hairpin along a dusty, stony track, undulating through patchy forest. After about 2km, fork L over the Rio Canedo stream, past Casera Vescovà (1734m) and up through patchy wood, keeping an eye out for elusive waymarking (path 561). Following the edge of a ski piste, you climb S to a broad saddle and dirt track on Col dei Baldi (E of the gondola car arrival station). Continue SE past Roa Bianca's white outcrop, and

L down to the farm settlement of Casera di Pioda to join the main route, after 2 hrs walking from Passo Staulanza.

From this rural scene with herds of cows and goats ringing their bells melodiously from surrounding pastures, AV1 (path 556) climbs determinedly SW up a well graded mule track (many short-cuts) on the rocky E shoulder of Cima Coldai, an outlier of the Civetta. This is a hugely popular route, bearing numerous walkers of all

Monte Pelmo from near the Coldai hut

shapes, sizes and dispositions on summer days. After two disappointing 'false tops', the path emerges suddenly at

1 hr 15 min – **RIFUGIO SONINO AL COLDAI** (2132m) – *tel. 0437-789160, CAI, 88 places, open mid-June to 20 Sept.*

The refuge is a good base for experienced climbers wishing to make an ascent of the Civetta (3220m), which extends S as a gigantic trident. It was first climbed by an Englishman called Tuckett in 1867, but for a long time afterwards the sheer N wall defied ascent. Two more English climbers – Raynor and Phillmore – overcame the technical difficulties and scaled this face in 1895, since when a plethora of routes have become established, earning the mountain immense popularity.

The Sentiero Tivan route from the refuge runs under the Civetta's E cliffs and onto the via normale and the Via Ferrata Alleghesi. Although an ascent of the peak is highly rewarding, it should only be attempted by experienced climbers, since there are long exposed stretches leading to a serious high-mountain environment.

Continue W up a small valley of white stone to cross Forcella Coldai (2191m) – a lip of land revealing the stunning turquoise waters of Lago Coldai, encircled by little stony beaches (good wild pitches). On the L, Monte Civetta's northern spurs of Torre Coldai and Torre di Alleghe send up rock buttresses and towers, while to the N stands the now distant Tofane, its cable-car top station just visible.

AV1 drops round the lake's shore and passes over Forcella Col Negro (2203m) before losing height and entering Val Civetta. (A higher narrower path cuts the scree flow and hugs the foot of the cliffs. If snow-free, it means a slight saving in terms of ups and downs.) In a succession of overhanging slabs, peaks and pinnacles, the W face of Monte Civetta towers 1200m overhead and extends for 7km in length – a marvellous sight which has been likened to huge organ pipes, the 'wall of walls',

Lago Coldai

• Variant to Rifugio Tissi: The path leaving R (N) leads in 30 min to Rifugio Attilio Tissi (2250m) – *tel. 0437-721644, CAI, 65 places, open 25 June to 20 Sept.* It stands close to the summit of Cima di Col Reàn (2281m), in a stunning spot opposite the Civetta and high above Lago di Alleghe. ➤

unique in the Alps. A hanging ice-field, the Cristallo, is suspended below the highest top.

Over undulating mountain terrain, the trail (on path 560) reaches

1 hr 30 min – **FORCELLA DI COL REÀN** (2107m). •

AV1 proceeds on down Val Civetta amidst a profusion of wild flowers, ignores paths off R and passes Col del Camp (1847m), whereupon it descends on a good mule track round the head of Valle di Foram, dominated by the square-cut tower of Torre Venezia (2337m). A short drop through pine trees leads to spacious

1 hr 30 min – **RIFUGIO VAZZOLER** (1714m) – *tel. 0437-660008, CAI, 80 places, open 20 June to 20 Sept. Lovely alpine botanical garden that boasts both common and rare specimens.*

Leaving N on the jeep track through thick forest, AV1 touches on Val dei Cantoni with the fantastic shapes of Torre Trieste (2458m) and Cima della Busazza (2894m)

ahead. As the track begins its zigzagging descent down Val Corpassa, take path 554 off the second hairpin.

The track S provides a suitable exit, dropping past homely *Capanna Trieste tel. 0437-660122, private, 20 places, open May to early Oct* then becoming a narrow road to Listolade, bar/restaurant and buses to Belluno and Alleghe.

You climb in mixed woodland to a minor *forcella*, watching carefully for waymarks, and continue over scree and rocks to gain the steep little

1 hr 30 min – **FORCELLA COL DELL'ORSO** (1823m).

➤ A goods lift from the village of Masaré enables supplies to be sent up. To rejoin the main route, follow the branch of 560 that slots back into AV1, uphill of Forcella di Col Reàn. 45 min extra are sufficient.

Starting with a short aided stretch along a flowered rock face then rising across boulders and thin pasture, AV1 turns abruptly L (SE) detouring the diminutive Casera del Camp to reach red earth layers and Forcella del Camp (1933m), a break in the spur thrown south from the Moiazza to Monte Framont. Dropping in a wide curve before the Moiazza's great S face, the trail (path 554) passes the start of the Via Ferrata Costantini (experienced and equipped climbers only) which heads up N into the

Rifugio Vazzoler ensconced in pine wood

Beneath the Moiazza, looking back to Forcella Col dell'Orso

scree and deep 'V' of cliffs to Bivacco G. Ghedini-Moiazza (2601m), before traversing the Moiazza's summit ridge E and returning S to Rifugio Carestiato. Your wooded and more modest line continues E for another 2km along the head of Val Framont, and a short detour R brings you also to the commanding outcrop that hosts

1 hr 40 min – **RIFUGIO B. CARESTIATO** (1839m) – *tel. 0437-62949, CAI, 34 places, open late June to late Sept. From the refuge are fine views down towards Agordo and over surrounding peaks, particularly the Tamer/San Sebastiano group to the E.*

Cutting off the first few zigzags, the route follows a wide track along and down through more forest, easily reaching the grassy and pastoral

40 min – **PASSO DURAN** (1601m) – *two privately-*

owned establishments: Rifugio Passo Duran 'C. Tomè' (tel. 0437-32034, 30 places, open start June to end Sept), good ambience, managed by an affable mountain guide; then hotel-like Rifugio S. Sebastiano (tel. 0437-6236035, 25 places, open start June to end Oct). No public transport from this road pass.

STAGE 3:
PASSO DURAN TO BELLUNO

The wildest and loneliest stretch on Alta Via 1 begins with a climb through pine forest and a traverse along to the rugged foot of the M. Tamer massif, an official variant passing round its other side on old hunting and forestry tracks. At Rifugio Pramperet, the route ascends to a rocky wilderness, an almost other-worldly landscape of bare, eroded limestone and dolomite, before dropping briefly to softer regions at the head of a lovely wooded valley and a homely refuge. The crossing of M. Schiara involves some technical difficulty, and those wishing to avoid it can walk out down the valley to a road and buses for Belluno. For walkers with climbing experience and a steady head, there is a thrilling descent down M. Schiara's south face on the Via Ferrata del Marmol. From the refuge at its base, a cascading torrent is followed down, in and out of woods, to the roadhead above Belluno, thence on roads through outskirts to the town centre and journey's end.

Note: This final section traverses high, committing terrain, far from roads, though with a scattering of good refuges. The traverse of Monte Schiara should be undertaken only by those with appropriate equipment, climbing experience and a good head for heights. Check the weather forecast before setting out and be prepared to turn back or use one of the many valley escape routes if necessary. Consider taking basic bivouac equipment to enable you to tackle the *via ferrata* at an early hour. The final aided stage is easily detoured by taking the variant via Rifugio Furio Bianchat (page 69).•

From Passo Duran, AV1 descends S on the road for about 2km to a bend at a torrent, which it crosses at

20 min – **PONTE DI CÀLEDA VECCHIA** (1493m) – *car parking space.*

• A different variant skirts the N and E flanks of the Tamer/San Sebastiano group, to rejoin AV1 at Rifugio Sommariva al Pramperet. This Zoldano Variant is summarised after the main route reaches the refuge.

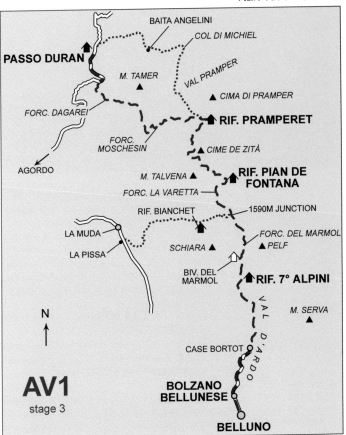

Path 543 breaks off here heading S, well waymarked and climbing through pine forest to Forcella Dagarei (1620m). There are distant views between trees of the Pale di San Martino SW on AV2 – from here seen side-on but actually a vast stony plateau.

The little path meanders along SE between 1600m and 1700m over boulder fields, meltwater ravines and scree, in and out of forest, to Malga Moschesin (1800m),

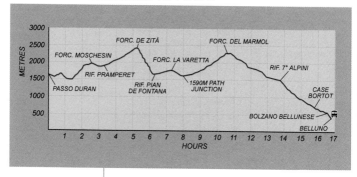

some deserted barns just beyond the indistinct saddle near Col Pan d'Orso. From here, a soundly constructed and well-graded old military mule track, reminiscent of the British packhorse roads, zigzags E up to a corner, where an unexpectedly fine view is met of Monte Talvena (2542m) and Cime de Zità (2411m) across the deep cleft of wild Val Clusa. Continue on past derelict World War I barracks, through a profusion of wild flowers to nearby

2 hrs 15 min – FORCELLA MOSCHESIN (1940m) – *The views are magnificent: behind, convoluted spires of limestone rise in tiers to Cima Moschesin, an outlier of Monte Tamer; to the N is Val Pramper and, if the weather is clear, the unmistakable shape of the Pelmo.*

• A feasible exit route drops N via a path then good tracks to Forno di Zoldo in Val Zoldana in 2 hrs 30 min ① 0437-787349, bus to Longarone and trains.

After a brief drop and fork R (E) away from the mule track (which continues down to Val Zoldana), AV1 coasts below the modest Cime de le Balanzole through a thin forest of springy dwarf mountain pines interspersed with showy martagon lilies. It leads to a meadowy crossroads at Pra' della Vedova, and a little further E lies

45 min – RIFUGIO SOMMARIVA AL PRAMPERET (1875m) – *tel. 337-528403 CAI, 40 places, open 20 June to 20 Sept. The modest refuge is a blend of the old and new extensions, its situation quiet and lonely.*•

Zoldano Variant from Passo Duran: this route (536) often follows old hunting and forestry trails and stays largely at 1500–1600m, circling the Tamer/San Sebastiano group to reach Rifugio Pramperet up the densely wooded Val Pramper.

On the trail above Rifugio Pramperet

From Passo Duran, follow the road N for a short stretch and take a mule track NE over torrent beds, across the big screes of Pian Grand and through wood to round La Coda (1665m). The path goes due S down over screes and through patchy forest past Forcella de le Caore (1725m) to arrive at Baita V. Angelini (1680m) *(emergency shelter only)*.

More forest leads over Col di Michiel (1491m) and a zigzag descent S to open ground in Val Pramper, threading along beneath the screes and vertical cliffs of Cima di

65

Cima Pramper over-shadows Rifugio Pramperet

Petorgnon and into Pian dei Palui. Here a mountain road is joined and followed for 1km via Malga di Pramper (1540m) for the climb to Pra' della Vedova and thence to Rifugio Pramperet. Allow 6 hrs 30 min from Passo Duran.

From the path junction at Pra' della Vedova, AV1 follows a good path (n.514) which climbs SW to the rocky Portela del Piazedel (2097m). Grassy slopes are strewn with boulders as the route ascends to a rough open area, interspersed with snow patches and much scree from the towering Cime de Zità (or Città) ridge above. Superb views open out over the Agordino mountains and the nearer Castello di Moschesin.

Threading S through rockfalls and zigzagging up steep, rocky grass, a small pass is reached with marvellous views down Val dei Erbandoi to the W. Beyond a grassy shoulder and tiered rocks, the rough path levels off to arrive at the

2 hrs – **FORCELLA DE ZITÀ SUD** (2395m) – *on the connecting ridge between Cime de Zità (2465m) and Monte Talvena (2542m).*

Ahead stretches a primordial, almost lunar landscape with denuded rock, boulders and scree, the glacially modelled Van de Zità; in places it resembles Yorkshire limestone pavements, but the scale is vast. Views are equally impressive – of Monte Talvena, the Pelf and the Schiara featuring the Gusela rock needle.

AV1 descends across this harsh environment where, incredibly, many endemic alpine flowers grow. Head down S below the rocky spine of Le Presòn on the L, keeping Monte Talvena's bulk to the R. A clear path negotiates broken rocks and a number of tortuous bends through crags and outcrops, punctuated by dolinas (extensive depressions or basins). Bearing SE and dropping steeply, it finally reaches pastureland at welcoming

1 hr – **RIFUGIO PIAN DE FONTANA** (1632m) – *tel. 335-6096819, CAI, 35 places, open mid-June to mid-Sept. In 1976 a barn here was converted to a permanent bivouac hut, Bivacco Renzo Dal Mas, named after a Belluno climber who died on the Marmolada. More recently it became a lovely refuge, greatly appreciated here.*

The trail (514) continues its relentless descent (almost 1000m since the Cime de Zità ridge), now over pasture to a path junction at 1424m. (Path 520, L, provides a rapid escape route, following the torrent down Val dei Ross to a rough road and Soffranco, bus stop, in Val Zoldana.) AV1 trends W then S, climbing more steeply in zigzags past a steep rock headwall to

1 hr – **FORCELLA LA VARETTA** (1701m) – *an idyllic spot in good weather, overlooking the depths of Val dei Ross to the E and the hugely impressive N face of the Schiara to the S, the prominent notch of Forcella Marmol through which AV1 passes is clearly visible. (A short distance W lies the deserted Casera la Varetta farmstead, useful shelter in emergency.)*

Now descend a small stony valley (good water source),

Monte Pelf and the Schiara seen from Van de Zità

re-emerge onto grassy slopes and contour round the head of Val Vescovà, maintaining height at around 1700m. After a steep climb is

40 min – 1590M PATH JUNCTION.

Note: The ensuing final push over the Schiara is far from a 'walk' in the normal sense of the word. Descending the S face involves some 500m of *via ferrata*, as the route cuts diagonally down the E end of the mountain. This well- known and sensational Via Ferrata del Marmol is waymarked and equipped with iron ladders of various sizes and lengths of anchored steel cable which, used in conjunction with a simple safeguarding technique that necessitates equipment (see Introduction), offer adequate protection. However, the descent is often very exposed, particularly in the lower sectors, and the mountain walker with little or no climbing experience would need a more expert companion or guide as well as the extra security of a rope. Bad weather or other factors might also militate against the crossing.

Variant avoiding the Schiara traverse: From the 1590m signed path junction, turn R to follow a well-marked path

(518), zigzagging down W, over a torrent then mostly in woods to Pian dei Gat (1245m) – a forest clearing dominated still by the magnificent N prospect of the Schiara massif. Here stands Rifugio Furio Bianchet *(tel. 0437-669226, CAI, 40 places, open beg. June to end Sept)*. Allow 45 min from the path junction.

The area is rich in geological interest, flora and fauna, all rigorously protected, and including chamois on surrounding crags and sometimes near the refuge itself.

From here in a further 1 hr 30 min a forestry road (no private vehicles) marked 503 leads down the attractive wooded Val Vescovà, short-cutting the last section to emerge at the main road for Belluno and a lovely waterfall La Pissa (449m) as well as a bus stop, 2.5km N of La Stanga which also has a café.

From the 1590m path junction, the main route (path 514) proceeds SE (watch carefully for waymarks in vegetation at first), up out of trees to the modest

30 min – **CASERA NERVILLE** (1641m).

The route lies unequivocally before you, a steep ravine between the Schiara and to the L the Pelf (2506m). Flowery levels are left behind for slabs and rocky outcrops, scree and snow patches. 700m of stiff ascent, arduous but nowhere especially difficult, leads to the

2 hrs – **FORCELLA DEL MARMOL** (2262m) – *a wild and airy place on the Schiara ridge.*

An apparently obvious way down is now confronted in the shape of the icy S gully, but it cannot be emphasised too strongly that this is both the incorrect line and a highly dangerous one. The CAI warn that there have been numerous accidents and several fatalities through people attempting a descent here.

Instead, look for paint flashes up the R wall towards the Schiara and, with care on the aided passages, arrive at

If you detoured the Schiara in order to explore the final section of AV1, take a local bus from Belluno to Bolzano Bellunese then walk up Val d'Ardo as far as Rifugio 7° Alpini at the foot of the Schiara rock wall.

20 min **BIVACCO DEL MARMOL 'SANDRO BOCCO'** (2266m) – *CAI, 9 places, permanently open. This small unsupervised metal shelter, installed in 1968 to the memory of a climber killed in a fall, offers a good starting point for climbs to the Schiara summit along the E ridge.*

There are wide views down into the Belluno valley and of surrounding peaks as the descent route begins in earnest on the Via Ferrata del Marmol – a dizzy, exposed 500m of ledges and gullies, corners, buttresses and airy traverses. Well marked and aided, it leads down to an overhanging cave called the Porton (1780m), from where easier grassy slopes drop to the conspicuous

3 hrs – **RIFUGIO 7° ALPINI** (1490m) – *tel. 0437-941631, CAI, 60 places, open mid-June to end Sept. The refuge, named 'Settimo Alpini' for an alpine battalion, is set against an amphitheatre of rock walls bearing numerous climbing routes and vie ferrate. Indeed, this S wall is considered by some to form an ideal introduction to* via ferrata *climbing.*

The final descent to Belluno and civilisation lies down the scenic valley of a torrent, a clear watercourse of pools and cascades, crossed several times on bridges. The path (501) clings in places to ledges cut into the ravine wall, at other times taking a line high above the torrent through delightful deciduous woods which conceal timid roe deer.

Just before the confluence of the two minor watercourses which become the Ardo, at Case Mariano (618m), you cross to the W side of the valley for the last time. A final level stretch joined by path n.506 concludes with your arrival at the tiny hamlet of

2 hrs – **CASE BORTOT** (694m) – *This characteristic cluster of diminutive old stone houses marks the end of the motorable road from Belluno. There is limited parking space and nothing in the way of facilities.*

The remaining walking along hilly lanes then on suburban roads might well prove more hazardous than the entire Alta Via just successfully negotiated! Compensations, however, include continuing wide views across Val d'Ardo to the distinctive cone of Monte Serva (2133m) rising above the first real farmsteads and settlements encountered since Passo Duran.

After walking 2.5km out to the first café-bar at the suburb of

45 min – **BOLZANO BELLUNESE** (541m) – no-one will object if you catch a bus the remaining 4km into

BELLUNO (400m) – *buses, trains, hotels, all supplies and services.* ① *0437-940083.*

The town is a fitting end to a classic Italian mountain route. Situated on the broad River Piave, it is a charming place, chief town of the province and surrounded by high mountain massifs: to the N the Duranno, Schiara, Monti del Sole, Pizzocco and the Vette Feltrine; to the S, a long pre-alpine chain culminates in Col Visentin (1763m), accessible by car or bus some of the way. In clear conditions the view from this isolated southern vantage point is unique, ranging across the broad mass of the Dolomite range in the N to the Venetian Lagoon in the S. Col Visentin has been adopted as an optional extension to AV1.

Half a day could be profitably spent seeing Belluno's sights, which include a number of buildings, piazzas and monuments of Renaissance and Venetian character. The Museo Civico contains fascinating Roman exhibits, and there are several shady public gardens beckoning to the travel-weary.

Over the roofs of Belluno's fine town houses, the great south wall of the Schiara, now 10km distant, still rises majestically, reminding you perhaps of the remarkable quality of the high-level walk just completed.

ALTA VIA 2

STAGE 1:
BRESSANONE TO PASSO GARDENA

Nearly 2000m above historic Bressanone, on the southern
fringe of the Tyrol, Alta Via 2 begins its journey southeast to
Rifugio Plose, crossing meadows and forest before climbing
a stony ravine to the first col. Against a stunning backcloth
of rock peaks and ridges in the Puez-Odle Nature Park, and
passing several refuges, the route crosses a steep *forcella* and
traverses rugged mountainsides onto a limestone tableland.
Rock pinnacles eroded into fantastic shapes lead down to
the winter skiing area of Passo Gardena.

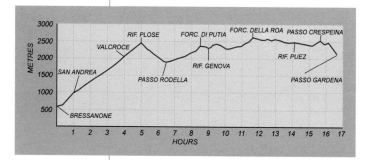

From Bressanone's railway station forecourt the eye is
drawn across Val d'Isarco, up beyond San Andrea's church
spire and intermediate levels of meadow and pine woods,
to the white Rifugio Plose and the Telegrafo summit,
2507m above sea level. Until this barrier is surmounted,
the limestone spires and crests of the Odle massif are
obscured by a greener, more rounded topography.

BRESSANONE (561m) – *all supplies/services; on road
and rail routes from the Brenner Pass.* ① *0472-836401.*

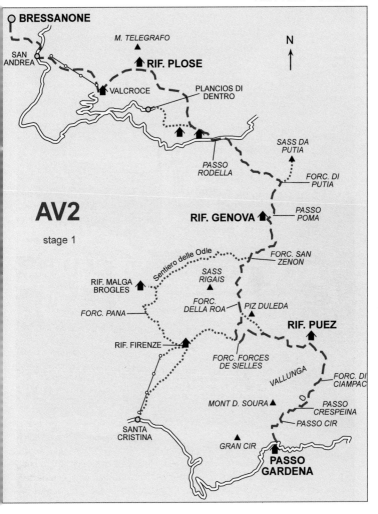

The historic town of Bressanone

Before leaving Bressanone, an important decision must be taken. The official start of Alta Via 2 is from Rifugio Plose, reached from the valley by a climb of some 1886m. This will take between 5 and 6 hours, a testing introduction to any walk. Whilst for the purist there may be no dilemma, the ascent being tackled with the necessary gusto, two alternatives for gaining this initial height do exist: one is a 21km drive on a good road to Valcroce (2040m, *rifugio*, car parking), thence by a footpath to Rifugio Plose. Another is to take the bus to San Andrea then the gondola car to Valcroce, continuing by path to the summit. Walkers should be forewarned, however, that while the bus service is guaranteed year-round, the gondola car does not usually commence running until the first week of July, concluding late September.

A third acceptable alternative entails taking a bus to Plancios di Dentro, avoiding Rifugio Plose and its bare surrounds pitted with telecommunications aerials and ski pistes altogether, and slotting into the itinerary at the minor junction Karer Kreuzl prior to Passo Rodella (see variant access at page 77).

For the ascent to the Plose on foot, starting from the town railway station take Viale Mozart opposite (E) through to the bridge over the Isarco river, grey-green with meltwater. Keep on to the nearby intersection and turn R as per signs for the Plose gondola car. About 10 min uphill, at a drinking fountain and old farm Kofler Hof, branch L for San Andrea. A quiet country lane (signed 7/8) climbs past a charming 13th-century manor house then passes L in front of a church before turning up into chestnut wood, from where you take a marked path L. This emerges in meadows dotted with traditional farmhouses bright with geraniums, and is joined by route 4/5 before cutting R across a grassy bank to join the road, where you go R towards the village of

Bressanone is an elegant and charming town with a history dating back more than 1000 years. It once belonged to the Roman province of Rhaetia, and has for centuries been a spiritual and cultural centre. Its surroundings are characterised by ancient churches, monasteries and notable buildings, with the old town itself still medieval in appearance. Shady, cobbled streets linked by narrow alleys and archways are pervaded by a distinct flavour of Austria, manifest in the rather upmarket prices, the strudel and cooked sausages, the leather breeches and feathered hats. Though this is Italy, the Germanic tongue prevails.

1 hr – **SAN ANDREA** (961m) – *provisions, hotels, bar/ restaurants, car parking, bus from Bressanone.*

San Andrea, ablaze with brightly coloured flowers in

gardens and window boxes, is dominated by its imposing church, with frescoes and a very tall, slender spire.

Your route (n.4/5) turns up L next to the Gasthof Gasserhof and its lovely shady beer garden, threading between houses old and new. A final stretch of wood leads to the gondola car station and bus stop.

A narrow surfaced lane behind the restaurant building is the start of n.17 for Valcroce. It quickly becomes a pretty path climbing steadily through conifer wood carpeted with bilberry shrubs, and is well signed at the many forks with intersecting forestry tracks and ski slopes. At a drinking fountain at 1450m, it forks L and narrows, the ensuing stretch occasionally obstructed by toppled trees. After a relentless zigzagging climb, it finally emerges to wide-ranging views at the Plose gondola car arrival station and

3 hrs – **VALCROCE** (2050m). A matter of metres downhill R is a beautifully placed, hospitable guesthouse, *Gasthof Geisler tel. 0472-521319, 45 places, open year-round, car parking nearby.*

The final stage in the climb to M. Telegrafo is via path 7, a constant climb NE through low shrub vegetation and grazing cows. From a scenic saddle it follows a fence and heads towards the white building of

1 hr – **RIFUGIO PLOSE** (2446m) – *tel. 0472-521333, CAI, 60 places, open 25 May to 1 Oct. Phone beforehand at beginning and end of season as the guardians go home at night if no guests are expected. Modern structure, more appropriate for winter skiers than summertime walkers.*

The 360° panorama is truly magnificent, including the Austrian Tyrol N, though the eye is drawn SE towards the dramatic rock spires of the Puez-Odle line-up, your next destination.

Alta Via 2 officially begins here. Set off along a track L of a chair-lift station, L at a bend to keep to the cliff edge and down to grassy flowered hillsides and various ski lifts. After 30 min a rough vehicle track is joined – keep L for 20 min, before cutting down R as per painted poles amongst ground-hugging alpenrose and juniper to emerge at another lane at

1 hr 10 min – **KARER KRUEZL PATH JUNCTION** (2000m) – *unusual old artistic crucifix.*

(5 min R is the charming private refuge *Schatzerhütte*, *tel. 0472-521343, 48 places, open mid-May to early Nov.*)

Variant access: Plancios di Dentro (1890m), the point with the Skihütte shown on maps (previously Sport Hotel), can be reached by bus from Bressanone. Leave the hotel and restaurant complex by walking R (E) along the road (8), which soon becomes a broad forestry track. It crosses a stream and climbs gently out above the tree line, past the turn-off for Schatzerhütte, to reach the Karer Kreuzl path junction in 30 min.

With a wonderful view SE to towering Sass de Putia, follow the track down and at a nearby sign turn R on a delightful path descending through pine forest and over a watercourse. The route continues on down towards the Halslhütte *(tel. 0472-521267, 9 places, open beg. June to late Oct)*, over several small streams, ignoring a path R to chalets, before finally reaching a metalled road at

20 min – **PASSO RODELLA** (1886m) – *This minor road pass divides the Plose group from the Putia massif and Puez group.*

Turning L, a signboard announcing the 'Puez Geisler Nature Park' is passed and the road followed for about 10 min. At a bend and another sign, path 4 is taken R through level forest over a bouldery torrent bed. The

The distant Tyrol from Forcella della Putia

conspicuous narrow valley ahead terminating in a pass, the Forcella di Putia, is your next goal, R of Sass de Putia, whose lower layers are a fascinating lesson in geology. After another torrent below a waterfall high to the R, it's a steady climb, joined by a path from the road below. At the foot of the steep little valley, the route crosses the torrent bed to its L bank. The ascent is relentless, but on a good path through rock and loose scree, with adjacent gullies often snow-choked well into summer. The shrill cry of marmots might be heard echoing from the enclosing cliffs. Soon, a grassy saddle and a crucifix appear ahead at

2 hrs – **FORCELLA DI PUTIA** – (2357m) – *a favourite spot for walkers and the starting point for the recommended climb up Sass de Putia (2875m), directly above to the N. The steep zigzag ascent entails a very exposed stretch equipped with metal cable on the final leg to the summit; however the western peak, only metres lower, is a straightforward walker's route, forking off at a saddle some 150m below the top. In either case allow 2 hrs return to the forcella. Views in both cases are immense.*

This pass, frequented by scavenging crows, provides a grand panorama. In the far SE rise the conspicuous peaks of the Tofane above Cortina on Alta Via 1; ahead to the S is the entire N wall of the Puez-Odle massif, with a glimpse of the distant Sella group's snowfields peeping above.

Take path 4 (S), contouring a hillside through small rocky outcrops, with the mountains of Alta Via 1 unfolding to

Approaching the Puez group from Forcella San Zenon

the E. From a crucifix at Passo Poma (2340m), drop round R to arrive at

30 min – **RIFUGIO GENOVA** (2297m) – *tel. 0472-840132, CAI, 80 places, open end June to mid-Oct. Lively popular hut, with good basic facilities, shower included.*

Walk E from the refuge on path 3, back up to Passo Poma through drifts of wild flowers, proceeding S past the Bronsoi outcrop. AV2 takes a rising traverse across steep stony hillside below a 2486m crest, where it turns R, slightly downhill. Ahead L stand the immensely impressive rock towers and snow-streaked screes of Punte del Puez. The conspicuous notch in the skyline to the S is Forcella della Roa, through which the route takes you.

The distant peaks of Alta Via 1 from the trail near Rifugio Genova

Meanwhile, as you meander above chalets set amongst idyllic pasture worthy of *Heidi*, contented cows chew the cud. Before long, the path arrives at a small pass with its almost obligatory crucifix

40 min – **FORCELLA SAN ZENON** (2293m) – *referred to*

as Kreuzjoch on some maps. From here a variant drops W, skirting the precipitous needles of the Odle group on the renowned Munkel Weg to give marvellous views. After an optional detour to delightful farm-cum-hut Rifugio Malga Brogles, a steep pass leads over to Rifugio Firenze, with the nearby gondola-lift giving access to the town of Santa Cristina. The variant rejoins the main route at Forcella Forces de Sielles (where details will be found – page 82).

AV2 (path 3) continues S from the path junction, descending a little, before starting to mount over chalk-white rocky slopes beneath Sass de l'Ega, crossing possible snow patches to round a rocky bluff (excellent view

Start of the climb to Forcella della Roa

Forcella della Roa

• Through the pass, a **variant path** (2c) for experienced climbers only leaves L, crossing a scree terrace near the foot of enclosing cliffs and emerging at Forcella Nives (2740m). From here, via exposed scrambles and traverses, not all aided, it is possible to climb to the dramatic ridge top of Piz Duleda (2909m). Back at Forcella Nives, traverse E to join the main route W of the Alpe del Puez.

N). The trail winds under the cliffs of Cresta di Longiarù and out across steep scree, whereafter extra care is needed. Beyond another rock outcrop lies a series of zigzags on very steep scree leading to the *forcella*. Most of the late-lying snow in this gully is avoidable, but early in the season frozen snow here, as elsewhere on these high routes, may dictate carrying an ice-axe or staff. At the top you reach

2 hrs – **FORCELLA DELLA ROA** (2617m). •

You leave Forcella della Roa, dropping S and ignoring the fork R down Val della Roa (unless a visit is to be paid to Rifugio Firenze or Santa Cristina). After rough but mainly level ground, you start to rise, meeting path 2 up from Rifugio Firenze and swinging up in zigzags E to the well-defined

1 hr – **FORCELLA FORCES DE SIELLES** (2505m).

Variant from Forcella San Zenon path junction: Path 33 drops W 300m in a series of loose zigzags to thin forest and a herd of cows at Malga San Zenon, otherwise known as Tschantschenonalm. Follow the rough road down for a further 100m, cutting bends to a stone bridge over an icy torrent. At a 1868m junction, turn up L into forest on path 35, a popular route known as Sentiero delle Odle or Adolf Munkel Weg after its ideator. It meanders charmingly past wild flowers in abundance, including alpine clematis and alpenrose, all the time beneath the massive screes and rock peaks of the Odle group which show signs of major avalanche activity. Ignore turn-offs to the lower farms, not to mention the strenuous climb to Forcella di Mesdì, and climb on in broken forest until a path L signed for Forcella Pana (n.6) – 1 hr 30 min this far.•

You climb S past huge boulders and zigzag up steep scree, gradually tending W towards the narrow *forcella*, hidden from view until the last leg. The well-graded path finally reaches the base of cliffs.

Rifugio Malga Brogles can be seen below in its meadow; your route tackles the steep gully, to the R of a chimney at first, then up rock steps and stones, aided by metal cables and timber traverses. There may be chamois around the cliffs as you emerge at the top of

1 hr 30 min – **FORCELLA PANA** – 2447m.

The contrast is astonishing, meadows stretching ahead to Val Gardena; beyond, the Sella group and the Marmolada.

On path 1, aim at a small lake and in 10 min arrive at the Troier Alm (meals, drinks, exceptionally fine crucifix). Skirt R of the tiny lake and continue in easy descent SE to

• A **detour** W is feasible – continuing on path 35, it's 50 min to the old-fashioned dairy farm Rifugio Malga Brogles (2045m) – *no phone, 32 places, open July to Sept*. A direct path departs from here for Forcella Pana.

Malga Brogles nestling beneath the Odle

45 min – **RIFUGIO FIRENZE** (2037m) – *tel. 0471-796307, CAI, 99 places, open 1 June to 15 Oct. A gondola-lift and track lead down to Santa Cristina, a smart, year-round resort (all supplies and services, ① 0471-793046).*

On path 2/3 pass L in front of the refuge and drop to cross a stony ravine, climbing out and across a flat area. Ahead L can be seen the jagged, shapely summits of the Odle, rising to Sass Rigais. The path bends R, round the rocky corner of Montejela and into a vast, almost rectangular amphitheatre of scree and cliffs. After climbing for almost 500m, fork R up to the now obvious connection with the main route coming in from the N, which is met just below Forcella Forces de Sielles. 1 hr 30 min from Rifugio Firenze.

Above Lago Crespeina looking back to Rifugio Puez and the path from Forcella Forces de Sielles

The main AV2 route now turns sharp L (N), climbing beneath rocky outcrops then contouring on more steep scree. After traversing this exposed fan of shattered mountainside, climb over a lip onto easier ground, drop down the rock-strewn Alpe del Puez and wind along

undulating terrain above cliffs on a natural platform high above glacier-shaped Vallunga. The trail bends S round a spur of Col di Puez (2725m), trends E again over stream beds and round a stony corner to a grassy saddle and the buildings of

1 hr 30 min – **RIFUGIO PUEZ** (2475m) – *tel. 0471-795265, CAI, 90 places, open 13 June to 10 Oct – access to Vallunga and the township of Selva in Val Gardena down path 1 (very steep at first). The refuge's isolated situation, far from jeep tracks and lacking the usual mechanised cableway, means supplies have to be brought in by costly helicopter. Clean and efficient establishment, with delicious strudel, though rather cramped sleeping quarters.*

You have reached the heart of the extraordinary Puez group, a vast limestone upland wilderness scattered with snow patches, a desolate and primitive landscape whose ancient origins are revealed in the many fossil remains, visible embedded in rock pavements. Gradients are gentle, but because significant landmarks are few and far between, waymarking should be watched for carefully in poor visibility.

Path 2 (with 4) leaves SE from the refuge, rounding the head of Vallunga and veering S (R) at a junction with path 15. About 1km after a small descent, the path divides at Forcella di Ciampac – 2366m (path 4 dropping SE to the waters of Lago di Ciampac and down to Colfosco in the valley). Your route (path 2) climbs gently SW over a vast stony plateau down to the vivid green waters of the tiny Lago di Crespeina, thereafter mounting steeply to the tall crucifix at

1 hr 30 min – **PASSO CRESPEINA** (2528m).

There is an exciting view ahead of the Sella massif, with its high square buttresses and snowfields, while down to the W, behind the monolithic Monte de Soura, lie the ski resorts of Val Gardena.

Evocative sculpted crucifix at Passo Crespeina

The trail winds through eroded limestone pinnacles above Val Gardena

The path descends to an enclosed depression at the head of the small Val Chedul – keep to the L upper line, contouring easily along scree. (Possible wild camping, meltwater.) A short, sharp climb through rocks leads up to Passo Cir (2466m).

After zigzags down the S side, the trail passes a remarkable forest of limestone spires (*campanili*), eroded into jagged, pocked pinnacles. You finally weave W down beneath the Pizzes da Cir cliffs into sloping meadows, past the timber hut of former Baita Clark in the shade of the Gran Cir, and down a gravel track past hotels to the road at

1 hr – **PASSO GARDENA** (2137m) – *Berghaus Frara tel. 0471-795225, 30 places, open beg. June to mid-Oct, showers and private rooms as well as dormitory. Also hotels, bar/restaurants, souvenirs, buses for Val Gardena and Bolzano (whence Bressanone), Corvara and on to Cortina, the Marmolada with Passo Pordoi; mostly twice daily. Wild camping is possible but there is no natural water source and the area is particularly busy during the day in high season.*

STAGE 2:
PASSO GARDENA TO PASSO DI SAN PELLEGRINO

A sensational gully ascent leads into the Sella group, a wild and barren rock upland fringed by vertical cliffs and gorges. Two refuges are passed and a climb can be made to Piz Boè (3152m). An exciting grain-smuggling path is followed past several huts, offering fine views of the glaciated Marmolada massif, with the loftiest summit in the whole of the Dolomites region. Experienced and equipped climbers can traverse the Forcella della Marmolada beneath the soaring west ridge, whilst walkers circle to the east, with the option of a three-stage cable-car ride to Punta Rocca on the Marmolada summit. Climbers' and walkers' routes converge at Fuchiade, a popular summer beauty spot just above Passo di San Pellegrino.

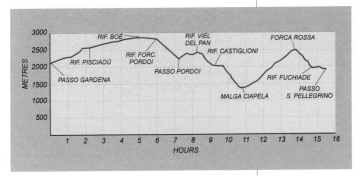

From Passo Gardena take path 666 behind Berghaus Frara for the Pisciadù and Boè refuges, contouring SE along stony slopes beneath the perpendicular walls of the Sella group. Unlikely though it seems at first, a manageable route does penetrate the massif – Val Setus. This narrow cleft gradually unfolds ahead R, its position

87

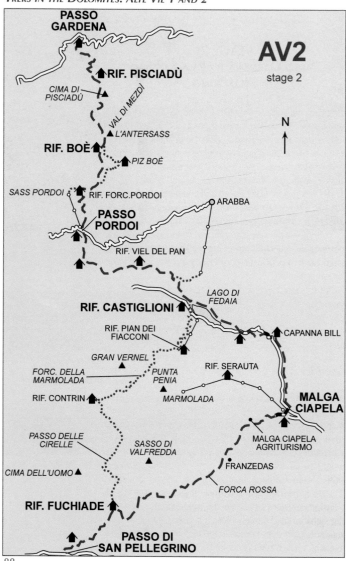

PASSO GARDENA

RIF. PISCIADÙ

CIMA DI PISCIADÙ

VAL DI MEZDI

AV2

stage 2

N

▲ *L'ANTERSASS*

RIF. BOÈ

▲ *PIZ BOÈ*

SASS PORDOI

RIF. FORC. PORDOI

○ ARABBA

PASSO PORDOI

RIF. VIEL DEL PAN

LAGO DI FEDAIA

RIF. CASTIGLIONI

RIF. PIAN DEI FIACCONI

▲ *GRAN VERNEL*

FORC. DELLA MARMOLADA

PUNTA PENIA

RIF. SERAUTA

▲ *MARMOLADA*

CAPANNA BILL

MALGA CIAPELA

RIF. CONTRIN

PASSO DELLE CIRELLE

▲ *SASSO DI VALFREDDA*

MALGA CIAPELA AGRITURISMO

CIMA DELL'UOMO ▲

• *FRANZEDAS*

FORCA ROSSA

RIF. FUCHIADE

PASSO DI SAN PELLEGRINO

The Sella massif and Passo Gardena

betrayed by a stony scar of a path ascending from the large car park at a road hairpin below.

Note: This is *via ferrata* country and is heavily patronised by enthusiasts of all shapes and sizes and levels of ability. One of the most popular of all – the Via Ferrata Tridentina – starts a little further E at a waterfall. Try to avoid ascending Val Setus late on a fine weekend afternoon, as it is likely to be filled with crocodiles of people descending the rock section, returning from the Tridentina.

Alta Via 2 turns into Val Setus, zigzagging uncompromisingly up scree and over old snowdrifts. The trail is well marked and there are airy views down to the map-like road snaking up to Passo Gardena. Early in the season, when this north-facing gully is still snow-filled, the climb would be on snow and ice, requiring the appropriate skills and hardware.

Up ahead the ravine narrows, curving to the L and crossing chutes swept by the odd rock fall, as per warning signs for 'caduta sassi'. The path steepens to a rocky scramble, aided by a well-anchored cable and spikes, but with no real difficulty.

Once clear of the rock section, the route bears L (SE) to a *forcella* and over a broad shelf beneath Sas da Lech to

2 hrs 15 min – **RIFUGIO PISCIADÙ** (2585m) – *tel. 0471-836292, CAI, 80 places, open late June to end Sept. Cavernous, well-run establishment.*

Rifugio Pisciadù and its lake

Go down round the L shore of little Lago di Pisciadù and proceed S across a long stretch of rugged mountainside over rock (aided), scree and inevitable snow patches. You are climbing Val Titus on path 666 along the W slopes of Cima Pisciadù (2985m).

There follows a somewhat steeper ascent over more snow and scree, round W and up onto Altopiano del Meisules, a barren lunar landscape. Though rich in ammonite fossils, the exposed rocky plateau here appears to be devoid of life, though summer sunshine reveals tiny alpine plants, lichens, insects and even birds. At a broad col, path 666 joins 649 coming up across the rocky upland from Passo di Sella via a *via ferrata* and Piz Selva. In a now S direction, cross l'Antersass either R via the more direct but exposed aided stretch or L via the longer but straightforward path. A descent over rough stony ground guided by cairns and poles finally leads to

3 hrs – **RIFUGIO BOÈ** (2873m) – *tel. 0471-847303, CAI, 70 places, open late June to late Sept.*

Just N of the refuge, beyond the helipad, path 651 from the desolate Val di Mesdì emerges from a dramatic ravine.

Ignoring 638 for Piz Boè (see following variant), the normal routing, path 627, rises over shallow-angled snowfields interspersed with stony ground until, topping a rise, the conspicuous Rifugio Maria and the cable-car top station are visible to the SW. A little to their L is Forcella Pordoi and its brand new hut, your next destination.

Continue following poles and cairns (especially useful in mist or early in the season when there is still extensive snow cover) across barren, undulating ground, then round over snowfields above a tiny frozen lake. Views E into Val Lasties are quite sensational – a miniature Grand Canyon.

Waymarking deviates from the customary red and white flashes according to the size and position of snowfields, but it is generally clear to follow.

A few rocky steps and the trail veers R, joining the descent from Piz Boè and contouring to

45 min – **RIFUGIO FORCELLA PORDOI** (2829m) – *tel.*

View from Piz Boè over the rugged Sella massif

The predecessor of Rifugio Forcella Pordoi

c/o 0462-767500 or cell phone 368-3557505 (reception often nil) private, 18 places, open 20 June to beg Oct. This hospitable newly constructed hut boasts showers and panoramic bedrooms.

Variant via Piz Boè: Instead of the normal route, a highly recommended alternative – weather and time permitting – is the traverse of Piz Boè, the most accessible 3000m+ summit in the whole of the Dolomites, with vast breathtaking views. Leave Rifugio Boè on path 638 bearing SE towards the rocky corner leading to Piz Boè up a scrambly ridge. The final section is aided, though not particularly exposed. A popular hut, *Capanna Fassa (tel. 0462-601723 private, sleeps 20, open 20 June to 20 Sept)*, shares the 3152m Piz Boè summit with a repeater. Alta Via 2 can be rejoined by descending the peak's SW ridge (still n.638), scrambly again in places at first. At the foot of the ridge corner the main route is encountered and Forcella Pordoi and its hut shortly gained. Allow 1 hr 30 min from Rifugio Boè.

AV2 now drops 600m, starting at the top of a steep scree gully, which can be awkwardly blocked with snow at the top. Helpful steps aid the initial stretch until the gradient eases off and the path broadens, before going madly zigzagging down the mountainside, across a grassy hill and down to arrive at

1 hr 15 min – **PASSO PORDOI** (2242m) – *bars, restaurants, hotels, telephone, souvenirs galore, buses for Arabba, Canazei, Passo Sella. Casa Alpina (tel. 0462-601279, 45 places, open beg. June to mid-Oct. Hotel-level accommodation). From Passo Pordoi a sombre military mausoleum (Ossario) commemorating the Austrian soldiers who lost their lives here during World War I lies 2km along a minor road to the E.*•

Leaving Passo Pordoi, you enter the Marmolada group and the volcanic Padon chain, first taking the celebrated Viel del Pan. In the 17th century the Venetian Republic became extremely jealous of its grain trade from southern Italy and prohibited the local population from selling maize flour. This route was used to smuggle grain through the Bellunese and Romansch valleys.

The wide path (n.601) begins behind Albergo Savoia, forking R before a small chapel and climbing easy slopes beneath 2538m Sass Beccè and above a noisy marmot colony. It is an extremely popular walk

• **Alternative descent:** An easier descent from Forcella Pordoi (depending on weather, energy levels and conscience) is to climb W (way-marked) to Rifugio Maria on Sass Pordoi (2952m). Here, too, meals and drinks (but no accommodation) may be obtained and Passo Pordoi reached effortlessly by cable-car late June to late Sept.

Grazing sheep opposite the Marmolada and its retreating glacier

and well signed, and quickly climbs to a grassy panoramic crest and past the well-located *Rifugio Baita Fredarola (tel. 0462-602072, privately owned, 36 places, open 20 June to end Sept.)*

A jeep track is followed E, undulating along the S flank of Col del Cuch with magnificent views across the deep Avisio valley to the glacier-bound Marmolada and adjacent Gran Vernel. These great peaks form a prodigious mountain barrier, which south-bound walkers need to cross or circumvent.

Contouring grassy hillsides thick with wild flowers, below marvellous volcanic formations akin to Easter Island statues, the track easily reaches stunningly situated

1 hr – **RIFUGIO VIEL DEL PAN** (2432m) – *tel. 0462-601720, privately owned, sleeps 15, open 20 June to 20*

Lago di Fedaia from the Viel del Pan, with the Civetta in the background

Sept, also May + Oct for meals and drinks. Simple but welcoming family-run hut with great meals.

Soon to the N, after the curiously squarish rock formation Sas Ciapel, before sight of them is lost, are good views back to Passo Pordoi and Piz Boè topping the Sella massif.

After about 2km of mainly level path, a junction is reached. The L fork continues above a line of rocky bluffs below the steep cliffs of Belvedere (2650m) and round NE to the hut and top station of a July–Sept cable-car from Arabba (① 0436-79130, hotels, provisions, restaurants, cafés, buses). However, Alta Via 2 takes the R fork, dropping in zigzags round the rocky bluffs to the W end of the lovely Lago di Fedaia. It is an artificial lake, and by the dam stands the

1 hr – **RIFUGIO CASTIGLIONI** (2044m) – *tel. 0462-601117, private, 50 places, open all year. Also known as Rifugio Marmolada. Accommodation here is in great demand – reservation advisable. A number of guest houses can be found in the vicinity. There are bus services both directions to Malga Ciapela and Canazei.*

The main walking route describes a wide arc to the E of the Marmolada, but an option for those with the necessary experience (and given suitable weather) crosses the Forcella della Marmolada. This is not an ordinary walking itinerary and requires at least some mountaineering skill and equipment: ice-axe, crampons and rope, high-factor sun screen and goggles. Naturally conditions vary from year to year, and may range from a straightforward traverse of snow-covered glacier early summer to a good 150m of exposed ice later on. This route is described first as far as Rifugio Fuchiade, near which the two alternatives rejoin, but the Marmolada is such a significant landmark to have reached that a little extra information would not go amiss.

The huge limestone massif, 1000m high along some of the 5km of its south face, is capped by the largest gla-

The Marmolada summit from the trail above Passo Pordoi

cier in the Eastern Alps. Its moraines carry the imprints of many fossils, while on the mountain itself there is a predominance of high, grey rock slabs and smooth vertical gullies.

The Marmolada was first attempted (unsuccessfully) in 1830 by Italian climbers from the Livinallongo valley and in 1860 by the English climber John Ball, who managed to reach Punta Rocca (3309m), the lower of the two summits. Four years later, Paul Grohmann from Austria, accompanied by Italian guides, reached Punta Penia itself (3340m).

During the spring of 1916, and again in the summer of 1917, the Marmolada witnessed fierce hand-to-hand fighting between Austrian and Italian troops. It was a perpetual contest for positional superiority, with action by small patrols over very difficult terrain, often in appalling weather conditions.

To escape enemy fire, the Austrians excavated an ingenious complex of galleries some 12km in total length, within the glacier itself: dubbed the 'City of Ice', it proved spacious enough to shelter a whole battalion. To individual acts of daring and heroism on both sides was added the constant threat from storm and avalanche which claimed many hundreds of lives, particularly in 1916. It is still possible today to find cave openings, the remnants of paths, commando posts and barracks on the mountains.

CLIMBERS' ROUTE

Cross the dam from Rifugio Castiglioni to the valley station of the glacier gondola lift. Either take this or climb S on path 606 skirting Col dei Boush and thence over rock and scree to reach

2 hrs (on foot) – **RIFUGIO PIAN DEI FIACCONI** (2626m) – *tel. 0462-601412, privately owned, 30 places, open late June to late Sept.*

From Pian dei Fiacconi it is necessary to descend first, losing considerable height, before the thin track veers W. The glacier has retreated since maps were surveyed, and the route now crosses glaciated rock, snow and ice patches at easy gradients in a corrie to where the NW

Near Punta Rocca, lower of Marmolada's two summits

crest of the Marmolada drops as a great sharp-edged ridge of rock. Skirt S round beneath this, then mount the steep glacier for about 150m and shattered rock (route depending on conditions) up to

3 hrs – FORCELLA DELLA MARMOLADA (2910m) – a narrow notch between Piccolo Vernel and the W ridge of Punta Penia (climbable from here on the Via Ferrata Marmolada).

There follows an aided 20m vertical rock descent down a narrow gully, then a big drop down extensive scree zigzags. Pass a junction with path 610, and keep R (W) over more scree and thin pasture down to

1 hr 30 min – RIFUGIO CONTRIN (2016m) – *tel. 0462-601101, privately owned, 130 places, open mid-June to late Sept. Managed by ANA, the historic Italian Alpine Forces Association.*

From the Malga Contrin dairy farm, a little E of the refuge, take path 607 at a junction, meandering S over torrent beds. After a short and steeper section, another path junction is reached at which you turn sharp L (SE) up a rising spur. In about 2km you arrive at a small col

(2440m) where a trail leaves L for Passo Ombrettola. Continue R (SW) on path 607 up a broad valley of fallen rock debris, in a dramatic setting where walkers are dwarfed, towards a gap in the skyline ahead

The vast scree basin of Val delle Cirelle

2 hrs – **PASSO DELLE CIRELLE** (2683m)

On a good path AV2 descends steep mobile scree (possible snow patches require care) with plenty of suitable short cuts. After a narrow passage by a large rock to the R, it zigzags L down stony slopes to a bouldery depression to become a winding path down flowery hillsides to a stream (suitable for wild camping). A good path through lush meadows leads to

1 hr 15 min – **RIFUGIO FUCHIADE** (1972m) – *tel. 0462-574281, privately owned, 18 places, open mid-June to end Sept. Comfortable upmarket guesthouse (only a handful of dormitory beds available) with a good reputation for typical local cuisine. Booking strongly suggested.*

WALKERS' ROUTE

(This section can be covered by bus if desired.) From Rifugio Castiglioni, follow the road along Lago di Fedaia's N shore, past a smaller lake beyond the dam, to reach Passo di Fedaia (2122m) and another private hut, Rifugio Passo Fedaia *(tel. 0437-722007, private, 18 places, open start June to end Sept.)*

AV2 now keeps to the right-hand side of the road to drop via Pian de Lobbia on a ski piste and descends beneath angled rock slabs under Sass del Mulo, and thence down to 1780m and the Capanna Bill hut *(tel. 0437-722100, private, 24 places, open July to Sept)*. Now it's mostly a matter of walking on grass verges the rest of the way to

1 hr 30 min – **MALGA CIAPELA** (1384m) – *hotels, bars, restaurants, car parking, campsite, limited provisions, buses. This smart, though small, tourist development makes an excellent base for exploring the Marmolada and peaks to the W and S, criss-crossed by numerous paths.•*

AV2 passes the cable-car entrance at Malga Ciapela, drops a little to a lane R (W) alongside the Pettorina torrent and passes a campsite. A popular cross-country ski route in winter, the surfaced lane (n.610) leads up through forest to the wooden farm buildings of

30 min – **MALGA CIAPELA AGRITURISMO** (1534m) – *dairy products, meals and refreshments only, car parking.*

Shortly after the parking area, continue up ahead on the broad, rough track climbing steadily. Where this veers decidedly R (NW) for Rifugio Falier turn L on 689 (signed Forca Rossa) – there is a fine view of the Marmolada's vast south wall leading E to Piz Serauta (3035m).

More relentless zigzags take you up through thinning forest (increasingly open views E to Monte Chegaris) until, just short of barns at Franzedas and before a 90° bend in the track to cross a stream, you turn up R.

The jeep track you have followed has obliterated much of the original mule track until now, but from here this well-constructed military way leads up across a

• The three-stage **cable-car** ascent to Rifugio Punta Rocca (3250m) near the Marmolada summit is highly recommended; although not cheap, it represents good value, for the ride up is sensational. Above Rifugio Serauta (2950m), the half-way station, the edge of the Marmolada glacier is crossed, and from the top station (meals, drinks, etc.) a snowy ridge leads west for some 200m, with exceptional far-reaching views in all directions, given good visibility. Information on temperature, wind speed and visibility is available, along with cable-car running times, at the valley station.

bouldery alp, close to the infant Pettorina, through more conifers and across earthy slopes, finally zigzagging SW as 694 up to the broad

2 hrs 30 min – **FORCA ROSSA** (2490m). *A strategic pass during World War I.*

Still heading SW, AV2 descends past reddish slopes, through undulating and rough stony pastures before slanting up a grassy ridge which it crosses lower down. Swinging round past several path intersections, with marvellous views S to the Pale di San Martino group, you join meadows and a motorable track at

1 hr – **RIFUGIO FUCHIADE** (1972m, see above for practical information), *where climbers' and walkers' routes are coincident.•*

From the refuge, follow the track down SW, keeping R at the nearby fork. After light wood on the last leg, you pass Albergo Miralago *(tel. 0462-573088, private, open year round except May and Nov)* adjacent to the diminutive Lago di Pozze, to arrive at

45 min – **PASSO DI SAN PELLEGRINO** (1919m) – *hotels, bar/restaurant, car parking, telephone, rare buses to Falcade ⓘ 0437-599241 and Moena in Val di Fassa ⓘ 0462-573122.*

• The **Valfredda** pasture valley lies beneath a wall of peaks, from (W to E) Cima dell'Uomo (3010m) to Sasso di Valfredda (3002m). It contains many old photogenic timber chalets and is a popular picnic destination with Italian families who drive up the track from Passo di San Pellegrino. Grassy meadows are ablaze with colourful wild flowers.

Emerald meadows and chalets in Valfredda, Pale di San Martino beyond

STAGE 3:
PASSO DI SAN PELLEGRINO TO PASSO CEREDA

Crossing boulder-strewn upland above a lake, AV2 drops to a road pass before commencing a particularly rugged section over the highest point on either Alta Via – a pass at 2932m. The walker is led through a landscape of incredible rock peaks and past a high refuge as the path, aided on several stretches, climbs to the Pale di San Martino plateau. This vast and ancient limestone tableland, once a coral lagoon, is transected by many paths radiating from a popular refuge and forms part of a nature reserve above the smart ski resort of San Martino di Castrozza. A stony descent is followed by rock ledges to a pass and arrival at another refuge, set by a mountain lake and surrounded by rock spires. Beyond the next rugged *forcella*, AV2 loses 1000m of altitude, passing a bivouac hut and reaching the last refuge on this stage, situated in dense forest. A steep, high passage and a traverse beneath crags and rock faces bring you down to meadows and thence to the road and farmland at Passo Cereda.

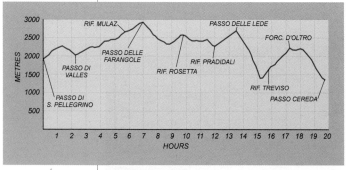

Passo di San Pellegrino has been developed for skiers and tourists and is paying the inevitable price in dese-

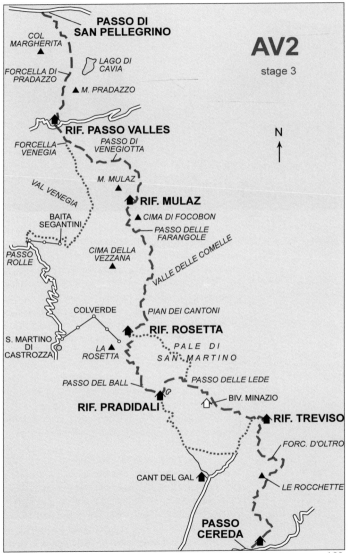

PASSO DI SAN PELLEGRINO

COL MARGHERITA ▲

FORCELLA DI PRADAZZO

LAGO DI CAVIA

▲ *M. PRADAZZO*

AV2

stage 3

N ↑

🏠 **RIF. PASSO VALLES**

FORCELLA VENEGIA

PASSO DI VENEGIOTTA

VAL VENEGIA

M. MULAZ ▲

🏠 **RIF. MULAZ**

▲ *CIMA DI FOCOBON*

— *PASSO DELLE FARANGOLE*

BAITA SEGANTINI

PASSO ROLLE

CIMA DELLA VEZZANA ▲

VALLE DELLE COMELLE

COLVERDE

PIAN DEI CANTONI

S. MARTINO DI CASTROZZA

LA ▲ *ROSETTA*

🏠 **RIF. ROSETTA**

PALE DI SAN MARTINO

PASSO DELLE LEDE

PASSO DEL BALL

🏠 **RIF. PRADIDALI**

△ *BIV. MINAZIO*

🏠 **RIF. TREVISO**

FORC. D'OLTRO

▲ *LE ROCCHETTE*

CANT DEL GAL 🏠

PASSO CEREDA 🏠

On the vast bare upland of Pale di San Martino

cration. A cable-car runs to the porphyry rock mass of Col Margherita (2550m), a singularly unattractive summit for these parts, and a new ski piste has been bull-dozed up to the col used by AV2 near Cima Pale di Gargol. The initial section as far as Passo di Valles is rather uninspiring but is difficult to avoid without a car: the odd Falcade bus from Passo di San Pellegrino can be used as far as the Passo Valles turn-off, but from there on it's 7km by road – hitchhiking is worth a try, though traffic may be light.

Opposite the track from Rifugio Fuchiade, leave the pass across a big car park on path 658, signed for Passo Valles. Bear L through marshy terrain and proceed up through thin bushy forest and under the cable-car. The path eventually turns sharp R and later L to climb more steeply on a dreary, steep ski piste through rock outcrops to arrive at a 2297m col.

Ahead lies a grassy upland strewn with large granite boulders and ski pistes – the Altipiano degli Zingari – and below you Lago di Cavia and its dam. In normal visibility there are no route-finding problems, but in mist watch carefully for waymarks. Leave the broad piste (which continues for Col Margherita) and turn off L as per cairns and red/white waymarking to proceed S over undulating terrain, eventually joining a motorable track at Forcella di Pradazzo (2220m). Amidst magnificent views ahead to the Pale di San Martino and with Rifugio Larese (meals and refreshments only) high above L, take

the road downhill winding S. Passing Malga Pradazzo on the last leg, it emerges at

Classic Dolomite scenery – Croda della Pala

2 hrs 15 min – **PASSO DI VALLES** (2031m) – *and marvellous, privately run Rifugio Passo Valles, tel. 0437-599136, 40 places, open all year except Nov. Reasonable rates for hotel-type rooms as well as dorm accommodation, not to mention generous meals. Also bar/restaurant, telephone, car parking and resident St. Bernard dog!*

AV2 (n.751) climbs SE from the pass, at first badly eroded then angling L up the slopes of Cima Valles (2305m). Ahead are the big red-sandstone striated cliffs of Cima Caladora (2313m), as you labour up to the first little pass

30 min – **FORCELLA VENEGIA** (2217m).

Variant: To bypass the following official sections entailing a series of steep and exposed tracts as far as Rifugio Rosetta, or in case of bad weather, a recommended option is to bail out at this point via path 749 which turns down R for pastoral Val Venegia. There you join a rough road leading S and climbing to the magnificently placed restaurant Baita Segantini. Then follows a brief descent on foot, chairlift or summer bus to Passo Rolle (a good 2 hrs this far) and then coach to San Martino di Castrozza, whence a return to the main route on the plateau via the Colverde gondola car then cable-car to Rifugio Rosetta.

Cimon della Pala at the head of Val Venegia

Bearing L, 751 follows the panoramic crest with wide-reaching views taking in the metamorphic Lagorai chain S, though overshadowed by the Pale di San Martino ahead, the line-up featuring Monte Mulaz (2906m), Cima di Val Grande (3038m) and the majestic Cimon della Pala (3184m), its hanging glacier fringed with green ice. On these grassy hillsides can be found heather, along with gentians and edelweiss galore. The route passes behind the crest of Cima Caladora and alongside

106

a tiny lake where, with luck, the walker will spot or hear the thriving marmots which inhabit this area, and maybe even a shy chamois.

AV2 descends shattered mountainside on an easy path and turns a rocky corner around to

45 min – **PASSO DI VENEGIOTTA** (2303m) – *There is further access R down to Malga Venegiotta in Val Venegia, hemmed in to the E by a breathtaking rampart of snow-streaked rock towers and walls.*

Going E on path 751, you climb up and round a rocky spur, crossing the steep N slopes of the Monte Mulaz ridge to the small Passo dei Fochetti di Focobon. (Junction with path 753 going E to Val Focobon.) There are magnificent panoramas N and E over Val Focobon, and the incredible campaniles (rock spires) of Cima del Focobon are progressively revealed to the S.

Descend R across a steep slope and on down with care over broken rock (loose guiding cables) in a circular depression above the cliffs and screes at the head of

Rifugio Mulaz in its magnificent setting at the foot of the Focobon peaks

Val Focobon. The route zigzags up to a small bowl-shaped valley, often snow-filled. Depending upon the quantity and disposition of the snow, the path takes a line L across it onto moraine and up via rusty-red rock gully (aided briefly) to a small grassy alp. Following way-marks, you traverse steep little gullies and terraces, no more than easy scrambles, finally ascending broad, ice-smoothed slabs (more cables) to the small Forcella Arduini (5 min detour E to scenic 2582m Sasso Arduini).

With the Focobon glacier and the fantastic rock profiles of Cima di Focobon (3056m) and Cima di Campido (3001m) now close at hand, a short drop followed by almost level terrain takes you to

• From the refuge's rocky platform, a well-marked and straightforward track climbs NNW to the panoramic summit of **Monte Mulaz** (2906m) in 45 min.

2 hrs 15 min – **RIFUGIO MULAZ** (2571m) – *tel. 0437-599420, CAI, 70 places, open 20 June to 20 Sept. The hut's full name is Rif. G. Volpi al Mulaz, named for the Venetian entrepreneur count who launched the city's mainland industrial development in the 1920s.* •

Amongst tracks radiating from here, AV2 looks rather unlikely a line. Indeed the following stretch – some 7km (4hrs) known as the Sentiero delle Farangole – to attain the Pale di San Martino plateau requires a steady head and secure movement. It traverses steep and loose ground in many places but is well waymarked, and most of the more exposed sections are provided with metal cables (though some may have worked loose during the winter). Early walkers may need an ice-axe for hardened snow, and normally right into July snow cover is the norm. Enquire at the refuge about conditions.

Note: those wishing to avoid the following strenuous traverse can take path 710 for Baita Segantini and Passo Rolle (2 hrs 30 min), continuing as per the preceding variant.

From the refuge, climb SW towards Passo del Mulaz (2619m), forking L at a sign on 703 and scrambling up extremely steep scree to a small gap in the NW crest of Cima di Focobon called Forcella Margherita (2655m). Now on the other side of the ridge above a wild amphitheatre, the clear-cut notch Passo delle Farangole is visible SSE. The path skirts the base of the Cima di Focobon and heads towards the Campanile di Focobon amidst a forest of amazing rock shapes and vast

expanses of snow. A sharp L up steep mobile scree takes you to the final aided stretch for the pass in the jagged crest above. Confidence and a sure step are essential as broken rock, boulders and snow patches are navigated,

Passo delle Farangole squeezed between towering peaks

109

with loose stones making the going decidedly tricky in places. Remember that dislodged material can be a hazard for those following! This is the highest point reached on the whole of AV1 and AV2 –

1 hr 15 min – **PASSO DELLE FARANGOLE** (2932m).

Through the pass, the ground drops away to unseen depths in Valle delle Comelle, which cuts a deep trench SW into the San Martino plateau. Descend a short snow-choked gully (aided) and, hugging the cliff at first, bear L over rock-strewn slopes enclosed between soaring precipices. Zigzag S down to the gently rounded basin piebald with snow and head for the AV2 markings on the R side of Val Grande. Proceeding S along rugged mountainside cloaked with bright wild flowers and blessed with a magnificent outlook, the clear waymarked path

Descending the aided passage from Passo delle Farangole

drops round the base of the Torcia di Val Grande campanile, and bears R into the circular hollow of Val Strutt, a good area for chamois and marmots (and an access path for Biv. Brunner).

The narrow trail, exposed in places and equipped with metal cable where necessary, contours along to the head of Valle delle Comelle above crags on a stony, grassy shelf. After countless minor ups and downs it finally drops to

2 hrs – **PIAN DEI CANTONI** (2313m), a key junction in Val delle Comelle. Path 704 rising from Gares is joined, climbing SE up the rocky valley head with no more technical difficulties. You soon emerge onto the vast lime-

stone tableland of the Altopiano delle Pale di San Martino, mounting successive rocky steps up to an old military track where you go R on 756 for

Rifugio Rosetta not far from the cable-car arrival station and Cima Rosetta

45 min – **RIFUGIO ROSETTA** (2581m) *aka Rif. G. Pedrotti, tel. 0439-68308, CAI, 80 places, open 20 June to 20 Sept. Recently renovated, it has retained its essential, though comfortable, alpine style, but offers memorable meals, not to mention hot showers. The qualified guide-manager is on hand for advice.*

1km SW stands the top station of the Rosetta cable-car (bar, meals). If you are hankering after haute-couture clothes, expensive perfumes and watches, the ride down to chic San Martino di Castrozza (① 0439-768867) is a must. Luckily for the walker on AV2, there are also banks, hotels, bars, restaurants, Post Office, chemist, food shops, a campsite and buses. The sensational cable-car takes you to Colverde, whence there is a gondola lift to the valley.

Slightly off route but well worth climbing – Cima della Rosetta

Beyond the Rosetta top station lies a slanting plane of rock leading easily to the summit crucifix of La Rosetta (2743m). If circumstances allow, an ascent (about 30 mins) is strongly urged, for views over the extraordinary

Pale di San Martino are vast, and high mountains can be seen in all directions. There are also vertiginous views down to San Martino over 1200m below, the western edge of the plateau being sheer and precipitous.

The Pale di San Marino is a dissected, rolling upland of grey limestone, edged with rock peaks – its geological origin the inner lagoon of a coral atoll. Even the Puez tableland already encountered is dwarfed by the scale here.

Early in the season, when the surface is still piebald with snow patches, there is no vestige of greenery as far as the eye can see, except in glimpses of distant valleys. Yet, close to, this unlikely habitat supports a host of miniature alpine flora. The tiny blooms flourish in crevices and little protected corners away from paths which radiate from Rifugio Rosetta.

Paths themselves, for all their signposting and way-marks, are only scratchings across this hard crust of land – they are discernible where the stone is a little broken and browned from the passage of boots and where snow is bisected by a dirty groove of steps, until it disappears under the summer sunshine. Special care is essential in conditions of low cloud or the swirling mists that creep in unexpectedly, severely limiting visibility.

From Rifugio Rosetta, AV2 (now path 702) is well signed S, first over undulating limestone following a water supply pipe as far as Passo di Val di Roda, then almost 300m of descent down many steep, stony zigzags built into the sheer cliff side, amidst bright alpine blooms.

The broad path rounds crags beneath Croda di Roda on a ledge to reach grassy Col delle Fede, before crossing a gully and possible snow patches. At 2270m, a path R (702) drops to the valley, whereas you follow 715 and soon follow a ledge cut into the rock face (aided for about 100m though not overly exposed), with Passo del Ball a conspicuous notch ahead. The final slopes are likely to be across snow, but quantities vary from year to year.

From Passo del Ball (2443m) the gradient is easier, down beneath the cliffs of Torre Pradidali (2553m) and round over a rocky bluff to

On the cable aided section climbing to Passo del Ball

2 hrs 15 min – **RIFUGIO PRADIDALI** (2278m) – *tel. 0439-64180 CAI, sleeps 64, open 20 June to 20 Sept.*

The refuge's interior is full of character, a dark womb of varnished timber with a glazed balcony overlooking a roughly circular basin bounded by screes, gullies and soaring rock towers. These summits are eroded into fantastic sharpened forms – the Campanile di Pradidali – and the whole mountain mass S from here is threaded by many *vie ferrate*.

From the refuge, an interesting variant leads to Rifugio Treviso by dropping into forested Val Canali, thus circumventing continuing high ground with a couple of tricky passages and offering a pleasant contrast of itinerary, especially in poor weather. Despite appearances, it actually entails less ascent/descent than the main route. Details appear when the main route reaches Rifugio Treviso.

Rifugio Pradidali merges with the rockscape, and backdrop of Sass Maor

AV2 now leads off N past sombre Lago Pradidali, surrounded by bright posies of yellow poppies, and climbs bleached rock to a signed junction where you fork R on path 711. Your route, now E marked by red paint splashes, scrambles up a gully, possibly snow-choked. It follows a rocky ledge to the edge of a stony terrace, then up steeper broken rock before the gradient levels off and you approach the narrow

1 hr 30 mins – **PASSO DELLE LEDE** (2695m).

Shortly before the pass, an alternative route comes in from
N. A short cut, it leaves Rif. Rosetta to head SE and climb
across the plateau via Passo Pradidali Basso then Passo della
Fradusta, whence an unnumbered path skirting the wild
head of the valley well above Rif. Pradidali. Only feasible
late season when the snow has melted and the route
becomes visible. Check on conditions before leaving Rif.
Rosetta.

Your path now descends, relentlessly and steeply, first
down a gully then SE across scree and rocks at the head
of Vallon delle Lede. Winding on down its L side to
grassy alps, you trend R and drop to a small bivouac hut,
invisible until the last moment –

Scattered remains of
a US military plane
that came down
here in 1957 litter
the area.

45 min – **BIVACCO CARLO MINAZIO** (2250m). *Always
open, 12 places, no facilities or water.*

Keeping still to the ravine's L side, heading towards Pala
dei Colombi's enclosing walls, AV2 crosses gullies down
steeper rock and boulder slopes to a junction at the edge
of thin forest. Keep straight ahead (E) on 711 down
through conifers to finally reach the floor of Val Canali at
1450m and cross the watercourse. A short climb and you
join the main access path 707 from Cant del Gal. A
relentless half-hour zigzagging climb past waterfalls in
dense beech and conifer wood brings you out at welcoming

1 hr 30 min – **RIFUGIO TREVISO** (1631m) – *tel. 0439-
62311, CAI, 40 places, open 20 June to end Sept. Hospitable old-style hut with creaky timber floors and a hot
shower.*

Variant from Rifugio Pradidali: Descend S on path 709,
zigzagging down the head of Val Pradidali, steep stretches
aided by guiding cables. Brilliant alpine flowers can be
observed here. Lower down are pine forest and easier

Upper Val Pradidali

gradients. Some 1 hr 30 min in descent, turn L as per sign-posting for Malga Canali and Rifugio Treviso (unless you prefer to drop a further 30 min to 1180m and the *Cant del Gal guesthouse tel. 0439-62997, 24 places, open year-round, restaurant, parking, bus to Fiera di Primiero ① 0439-62407 and shops*). A delightful undulating path through shady wood leads around NE for Malga Canali (1302m, meals) in a lovely setting. After the parking area, a track (707) leads N up Val Canali to cross the water-course R and start the climb E, soon joined by the main AV2 route for Rifugio Treviso. 3 hrs 15 min in all.

Note: For those wishing to avoid the following steep traverse of Forcella d'Oltro, descend the road in Val Canali, taking path 738 on the L (E) near a shrine (a short distance uphill of the Park Visitors' Centre at Villa Welsburg) and climb round the ridge's S end to reach the main road just W of Passo Cereda. Buses can be used from Cant del Gal.

AV2 continues S from Rifugio Treviso as path 718, undu-lating through dwarf conifers and crossing several torrent beds. After a path junction it begins a relentless ascent E, leaving the upper limit of trees and climbing over rocks and scree, up towards the well-defined *forcella* in the

117

ridge wall ahead. The approaches are steep but problem-free, among boulders and on stony grass, leading to

1 hr 30 min – **FORCELLA D'OLTRO** (2229m) – featuring an unusual point of rock. The ridge you are crossing is quite narrow so that views from the *forcella* extend W and E over valleys far below.

Still on tricky terrain requiring care, follow way-marking E for approximately 200m, forking sharp R (SW) and soon beginning to ascend again along beneath the crags and rock faces of Cima d'Oltro, Le Rocchette and Monte Feltraio for about 2km. The path narrows and encounters several steep gullies with exposed segments, not to mention carpets of edelweiss.

After innumerable ups and downs, at a small valley head in a region of oddly shaped rocks the path veers SE and climbs to a little gap, passing thence to the R of a small rock tower (Campanile de Regade). A descent over stony and grassy slopes offers views ahead opening out to Piz di Sagron (2486m) and Sass de Mura (2547m).

Having negotiated the knee-jarring steep slope, you reach woods, pass a steep gully choked with clay-smeared boulders and emerge at flowery meadows and a good motorable track. Turn R and in 1km arrive at the main road and

2 hrs 30 min – **PASSO CEREDA** (1361m) – *and Rifugio Cereda, tel. 0439-65030, privately owned, 65 places, open all year except Nov. On the main road between Gosaldo and Fiera di Primiero – buses both directions.*

Unlike other major road passes so far encountered, Passo Cereda is agricultural in character, though winter snow cover brings a new lease of life to the area in the form of skiing – cross-country for the most part.

STAGE 4:
PASSO CEREDA TO FELTRE

The final stage traverses the Vette Feltrine, at the southern extremity of the Dolomites. It is solitary, wild country, largely waterless but surprisingly vegetated, especially on south-facing slopes. Leaving the village of Mattiuzzi, you climb past the scene of a major landslip to a well-appointed bivouac hut. The route threads along beneath mountain walls, passing large caves before arriving at the first of only two refuges in this stage. Following a ridge honeycombed with wartime tunnels, it climbs to the summit of Sasso Scarnia and descends towards the Piazza del Diavolo, an extraordinary glacially sculpted area of huge boulders which is also rich in wildlife: one of reserves that come under the vast Parco Nazionale Dolomiti Bellunesi. A broad track and easier gradients lead to the final mountain pass and the second refuge, whereafter an old military road drops steadily to Passo Croce d'Aune and the heights above Pedavena, renowned for its brewery. It is then but a short distance to the old walled town of Feltre, with its Renaissance architecture and flavours of the Veneto plain, which stretches south towards the Adriatic Sea.

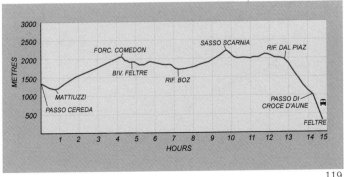

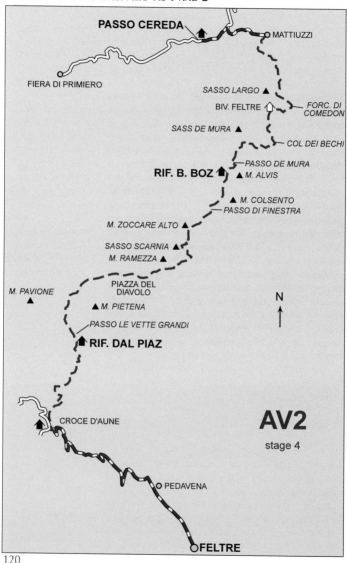

PASSO CEREDA

○ MATTIUZZI

FIERA DI PRIMIERO ○

SASSO LARGO ▲

BIV. FELTRE △

FORC. DI COMEDON

SASS DE MURA ▲

—— COL DEI BECHI

—— PASSO DE MURA

RIF. B. BOZ ▲ *M. ALVIS*

▲ *M. COLSENTO*
—— PASSO DI FINESTRA

M. ZOCCARE ALTO ▲

SASSO SCARNIA ▲

M. RAMEZZA ▲

PIAZZA DEL DIAVOLO

M. PAVIONE ▲

▲ *M. PIETENA*

N
↑

PASSO LE VETTE GRANDI

RIF. DAL PIAZ

CROCE D'AUNE

AV2

stage 4

○ PEDAVENA

○ **FELTRE**

Some believe that this stage is an afterthought, simply a device to bring the route to its conclusion at a sizeable town worthy of nomination as the southern terminus. However, the range forms an interesting contrast with those already walked through and thus avoids more repetition. Even though it maintains height at around 2000m, the path transects mountainsides often covered with scrub and vegetation or meadows thick with wild flowers.

The crossing will take about three days, and since there are only two refuges and one bivouac hut, walkers should pause and take stock. Safe descents from the massif may only be made in about three places, so if the weather threatens (and it tends to be less stable here, close to damp winds rising from the Veneto plain), escape from high ground can be problematic. If these or other reasons indicate that discretion may be the better part of valour, AV2 can be finished here at Passo Cereda, and Feltre visited by road if desired.

On the other hand, those intending to see the route through should consider carrying adequate provisions and possible bivouac gear too. Surface water is very scarce and supplies will need to be carried quite extensively. As with the final stage of AV1, weigh up all factors carefully before setting out and check the weather forecast.

From Passo Cereda, head E keeping to the main road for 1.5km and turn sharp R on a road through woods to the hamlet of

45 min – **MATTIUZZI** (1201m).

Past the church then playing fields, AV2 waymarks follow the road S, taking a track (801) off R at a bend. Zigzag up across meadows and in forest, with impressive views ahead of Piz di Sagron. About 40 min up from Mattiuzzi, a deep boulder-choked ravine is reached. Proceed along the L stony bank towards a narrow gap. Ongoing landslips and rock falls have led to several detours here, the path rerouted across the debris and made secure by a

Note: This final stage of AV2 comprises a trek across the largely unfrequented and remote Feltre Dolomites. Summits range between 2000m and 2300m, very rugged and steep on their north sides but sloping gently to the south into a vast upland dotted with great grassy hollows. Often these contain isolated monoliths or large rock slabs created by the action of ice over thousands of years.

long fixed cable. Great care is still needed in bad weather, especially after heavy storms, when more loose material is prone to movement.

Beyond, AV2 continues on a marked path, skirting rock walls R and aiming at a high, narrow pass reached up 200m of more difficult loose ground, including the traverse of a steep, slippery cliff, aided where necessary. This leads out to an old smuggler's pass

3 hrs 30 min – **FORCELLA DI COMEDON** (2067m).

A short descent R (SW) negotiates a secondary saddle and a rough gully (possible frozen snow) down to the grassy Pian della Regina. A brief climb takes you to the buildings of

30 min – **BIVACCO FELTRE** (1930m) – *The two corrugated-iron constructions, though unsupervised, make for a well-appointed bivouac hut, with 15 beds complete with mattresses and blankets in various stages of wear and tear, then a generous kitchen area with tables and chairs but no stove. Water close by.*

The well-marked trail (801) drops S across a flowery basin and winds up steeper stony slopes beneath contorted rock strata to Col dei Bechi (1960m). There are stunning views of the S wall of Sass de Mura, along the base of which AV2 finds its serpentine way W on the Troi dei Caserin ('dairy herders' path').

This is difficult ground, a little exposed and aided in places where extra care is needed, but the magnificent setting makes it worthwhile, and brilliant wild flowers stand out against the stark rock. Some large caves offer shelter in case of deteriorating weather and are interesting features. Before long the going gets somewhat easier on grassy slopes to the Passo de Mura (1867m). In less than 1km, Passo Alvis is reached (good escape path drops L (E) on path 811 via abandoned Malga Alvis to Albergo Alpino Boz in Val Canzoi), whereafter the route drops westwards to Malga Nevetta and

2 hrs 30 min – **RIFUGIO BRUNO BOZ** (1718m) – *tel. 0439-64448, CAI, 36 places, open 20 June to end Sept, Oct weekends. Offering simple facilities and patronised almost exclusively by walkers on AV2, this home-style establishment serves local dairy products.*

Bivacco Feltre makes for a comfortable stopover

123

If necessary, the village of Imer – buses and all services – in Val Noana can be reached on path 727, joining a stony track SW to Rif. Fonteghi, thence surfaced road.

Despite the lush appearance of vegetation, surface water is scarce on the next section and it is wise to carry a good supply.

AV2 (path 801) continues up to the Monte Colsento ridge, then SW along it to

40 min – **PASSO DI FINESTRA** (1766m) – *a depression between Monte Colsento and Monte Zoccare Alto. There is an electricity pylon nearby, an incongruous reminder of civilisation.*

Watching out for waymarks, continue S for a few metres but then leave path 805 (which descends steeply SE to Val Canzoi) and zigzag up R to just below the crest of Monte Zoccare Alto. Keeping under the ridge top, AV2 follows an artificial ledge cut into the rock (steel cable in places). The ridge itself is pierced by tunnels dating from World War I when these mountains, along with many others in the Dolomites, were the scene of fierce fighting between Austrian and Italian troops. They were re-used in the later conflict by partisan groups.

Sasso Scarnia (2226m) presents a wild and rugged prospect and your route zig-zags from a spur up steep steps cut into the rock itself. An aided stretch along the summit brings you out under the NE side at a broad shoulder, from which the path climbs beneath great cliffs, amongst huge boulders, before dropping across a gap and hugging the base of an overhang.

Now on the southern slopes of Sasso Scarnia, proceed along past rock towers and gullies and interestingly jointed rock walls until eventually a track is met coming in from the L (from Forcella Scarnia). Having crossed an area of lilies and joined an old military mule track, AV2 passes more rough ground and reaches a saddle SSW of Monte Ramezza.

Here begins a permitted deviation from the path, signed at a boulder L, to visit the Busa de Giàzz or the Giazzera di Ramezza, a massive cave containing a cone of snow and ice, once used to supply the brewery at Pedavena and the town of Feltre with ice. Ice-axe, rope and crampons are needed for a full exploration of the cave. Allow 20 min each way to reach it and respect the nature reserve rules by keeping to the waymarked path.

AV2 continues, almost level, along the Costa Alpe Ramezza, then climbs R over the crest, with a very exposed section on the N side high above the depths of Val Noana (care needed). The trail turns SW, traversing the uppermost perimeter of the boulder-strewn Piazza del Diavolo. The disorderly flow of huge stone blocks seems to have originated in a landslide; in any event, it is a most unusual place, the silence accentuating its unworldly appearance.

This is a special protected nature reserve, also part of the Parco Nazionale Dolomiti Bellunesi. Anything which could alter or disturb the habitat is prohibited. There is great scientific interest in this area, especially amongst botanists, and such an ancient landscape, unaltered by human settlement, deserves very special consideration.

After crossing a steep rock face beneath M. Pietena (2194m), you come round on scree, past curiously formed stones reminiscent of ancient monuments, and are joined by a broader track to a flat and grassy pass. The mule track winds down into a bowl of meadows surrounded by crags and scree and rich in flora. Below, near the sizeable mountain farm buildings, is the only spring since Rifugio Bruno Boz.

Becoming level, the track passes a path junction R (817) to Monte Pavione, then leads on S climbing gently to the final high pass on AV2 – Passo Le Vette Grandi (1994m). From here, the panorama ahead is unequivocally a lowland one over the valley of the River Piave and the green pre-alps beyond. Just below the pass stands

Passo delle Vette Grandi in early summer

5 hrs 30 min – **RIFUGIO DAL PIAZ** (1993m) – *tel. 0439-9065, CAI, 36 places, open 20 June to 30 Sept.*

A recommended extra excursion for breathtaking views leads to Monte Pavione, the green pyramid NW of the hut, and the highest point in the Alpe Feltrine at 2335m. The most direct route is via signed path 817, which forks off from Passo Le Vette Grandi to follow narrow ridges. 2 hrs 30 mins for the round trip.

The fascinating old military road (801) twists S, its bends short-cut for the walker amidst extraordinary spreads of wild flowers dominated by bear's-ear on rock outcrops and pheasant's-eye narcissus in the meadows. Dropping on a rough and tiring stony stretch through woods you emerge at a water trough and turn R along the road for

1 hr 30 min – **PASSO DI CROCE D'AUNE** (1015m) – *hotels, bars, buses for Pedavena and Feltre.*

In the absence of a bus, the best option is to hitchhike

the 9km SW down to Pedavena (346m) which boasts a brewery and adjoining park, a smattering of hotels and frequent bus services covering the remaining 3km to the centre of

FELTRE (325m) – *hotels, railway station, coach services to Trento and Belluno, all supplies and services.* ⓘ *0439-2540.*

Feltre is an unpretentious, very Italian town, notably less tourist-conscious than Belluno, its counterpart on AV1. The old town, still surrounded by walls and dominated by its castle in an enclave of Renaissance architecture, has been destroyed and rebuilt many times in its chequered history. There are old churches, a modest civic museum with paintings and sculptures, a theatre, a university institute of modern languages and the fascinating Galleria Carlo Rizzarda, dedicated to wrought-iron work.

A visit to the tourist office will be rewarded with AV2 souvenir badges and a chance to contemplate on the long, high mountain route stretching back in time and distance to Bressanone and the Plose summit, where it all began.

The historic town of Feltre and the conclusion of AV2

GLOSSARY

acqua (non) potabile	(non) drinkable water
aiuto!	help!
albergo	hotel
alpinistico	for climbers
alta via	high level mountain route
altipiano	high tableland
aperto	open
autostrada	toll-paying motorway
bivacco	bivouac hut (no guardian but basic equipment)
cabinovia	gondola car lift
caduta sassi	rock falls
campanile	rock spire (literally 'church steeple')
campeggio	camping
carta geografica	map
casera	small mountain hut of wood or stone
caserma	barracks
cengia	ledge
chiuso	closed
cima	mountain summit
col	mountain summit, usually subsidiary
corda metallica	metal cable (ie aided route)
croce	cross
destra	right (direction)
est, oriente	east
fermata dell'autobus	bus stop
fiume	river
forcella (forc.)	narrow saddle between higher grounds
funivia	cable-car
galleria	tunnel
ghiacciaio	glacier
grande	large
gruppo	mountain group
lago	lake
malga	mountain farm (if occupied may provide dairy foods)
mezzo	middle
molino/mulino	mill

monte	mountain
nevaio	snow field
nord, settentrione	north
nuovo percorso	new routing
ometto	cairn
ovest, occidente	west
passo	mountain pass or saddle
pericolo	danger
pian	stretch of level ground
piccolo	small
ponte	bridge
porta	small mountain pass
previsioni del tempo	weather forecast
punta	mountain peak
recapito postale	postal address
rifugio	manned mountain refuge
rio, torrente	mountain stream
rotabile	road
sasso	boulder or rocky peak
scarpone da montagne	hiking boot
seggiovia	chair lift
sella	saddle
sentiero	path
sinistra	left (direction)
sorgente	spring (water source)
stazione ferroviaria	railway station
strada	road
sud, meridione	south
tappa	stage or leg (in a journey)
telecabina	gondola lift
telefono	telephone
torre	tower
val, valle	valley
vedretta	hanging glacier
via ferrata	aided climbing route
via normale	normal ascent route for climbers

AV1 Route Summary

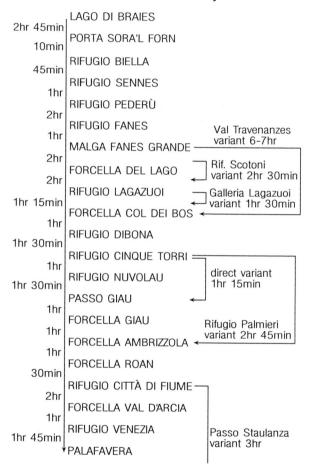

LAGO DI BRAIES
2hr 45min
PORTA SORA'L FORN
10min
RIFUGIO BIELLA
45min
RIFUGIO SENNES
1hr
RIFUGIO PEDERÙ
2hr
RIFUGIO FANES
1hr
MALGA FANES GRANDE ——— Val Travenanzes
variant 6-7hr
2hr
FORCELLA DEL LAGO ——— Rif. Scotoni
variant 2hr 30min
2hr
RIFUGIO LAGAZUOI ——— Galleria Lagazuoi
1hr 15min
variant 1hr 30min
FORCELLA COL DEI BOS ◄———
1hr
RIFUGIO DIBONA
1hr 30min
RIFUGIO CINQUE TORRI ═══
1hr
RIFUGIO NUVOLAU
direct variant
1hr 30min
1hr 15min
PASSO GIAU ◄———
1hr
FORCELLA GIAU
1hr
Rifugio Palmieri
variant 2hr 45min
FORCELLA AMBRIZZOLA ◄———
1hr
FORCELLA ROAN
30min
RIFUGIO CITTÀ DI FIUME ———
2hr
FORCELLA VAL D'ARCIA
1hr
RIFUGIO VENEZIA
1hr 45min
Passo Staulanza
variant 3hr
▼PALAFAVERA

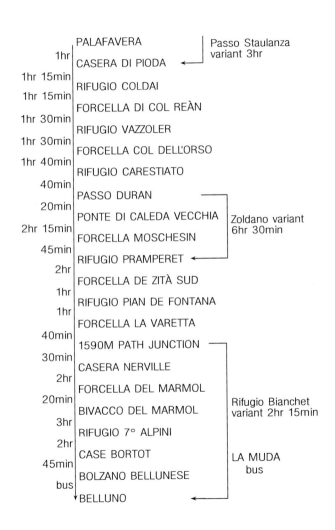

	PALAFAVERA	
1hr		Passo Staulanza
	CASERA DI PIODA ←	variant 3hr
1hr 15min		
	RIFUGIO COLDAI	
1hr 15min		
	FORCELLA DI COL REÀN	
1hr 30min		
	RIFUGIO VAZZOLER	
1hr 30min		
	FORCELLA COL DELL'ORSO	
1hr 40min		
	RIFUGIO CARESTIATO	
40min		
	PASSO DURAN	
20min		
	PONTE DI CALEDA VECCHIA	Zoldano variant
2hr 15min		6hr 30min
	FORCELLA MOSCHESIN	
45min		
	RIFUGIO PRAMPERET ←	
2hr		
	FORCELLA DE ZITÀ SUD	
1hr		
	RIFUGIO PIAN DE FONTANA	
1hr		
	FORCELLA LA VARETTA	
40min		
	1590M PATH JUNCTION	
30min		
	CASERA NERVILLE	
2hr		
	FORCELLA DEL MARMOL	
20min		
	BIVACCO DEL MARMOL	Rifugio Bianchet
3hr		variant 2hr 15min
	RIFUGIO 7° ALPINI	
2hr		
	CASE BORTOT	LA MUDA
45min		bus
	BOLZANO BELLUNESE	
bus		
↓	BELLUNO ←	

AV2 Route Summary

	BRESSANONE
1hr	
	SAN ANDREA
3hr	
	VALCROCE
1hr	
	RIFUGIO PLOSE
1hr 10min	
	KARER KRUEZL PATH J'N
20min	
	PASSO RODELLA
2hr	
	FORCELLA DI PUTIA
30min	
	RIFUGIO GENOVA
40min	
	FORCELLA SAN ZENON
2hr	
	FORCELLA DELLA ROA
1hr	
	FORC. FORCES DE SIELLES
1hr 30min	
	RIFUGIO PUEZ
1hr 30min	
	PASSO CRESPEINA
1hr	
	PASSO GARDENA
2hr 15min	
	RIFUGIO PISCIADÙ
3hr	
	RIFUGIO BOÈ
45min	
	RIFUGIO FORC. PORDOI
1hr 15min	
	PASSO PORDOI
1hr	
	RIFUGIO VIEL DEL PAN
1hr	
	RIFUGIO CASTIGLIONI
1hr 30min	
	MALGA CIAPELA
30min	
	MALGA CIAPELA AGRIT.
2hr 30min	
	FORCA ROSSA
1hr	
	RIFUGIO FUCHIADE

Sentiero Odle
variant 5hr 15min

Piz Boè variant
1hr 30min

CLIMBERS' ROUTE
9hr 45min

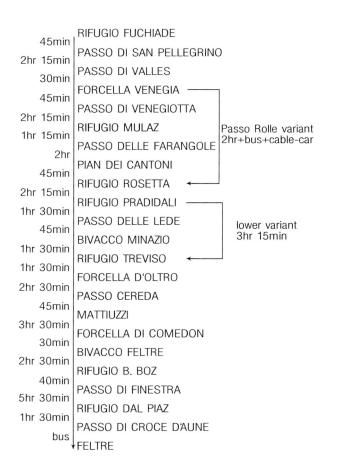

	RIFUGIO FUCHIADE
45min	
	PASSO DI SAN PELLEGRINO
2hr 15min	
	PASSO DI VALLES
30min	
	FORCELLA VENEGIA
45min	
	PASSO DI VENEGIOTTA
2hr 15min	
	RIFUGIO MULAZ
1hr 15min	Passo Rolle variant
	PASSO DELLE FARANGOLE 2hr+bus+cable-car
2hr	
	PIAN DEI CANTONI
45min	
	RIFUGIO ROSETTA
2hr 15min	
	RIFUGIO PRADIDALI
1hr 30min	
	PASSO DELLE LEDE lower variant
45min	3hr 15min
	BIVACCO MINAZIO
1hr 30min	
	RIFUGIO TREVISO
1hr 30min	
	FORCELLA D'OLTRO
2hr 30min	
	PASSO CEREDA
45min	
	MATTIUZZI
3hr 30min	
	FORCELLA DI COMEDON
30min	
	BIVACCO FELTRE
2hr 30min	
	RIFUGIO B. BOZ
40min	
	PASSO DI FINESTRA
5hr 30min	
	RIFUGIO DAL PIAZ
1hr 30min	
	PASSO DI CROCE D'AUNE
bus	FELTRE

REFUGE STAMPS

REFUGE STAMPS

REFUGE STAMPS

REFUGE STAMPS

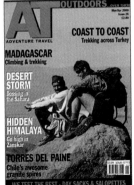

LISTING OF CICERONE GUIDES

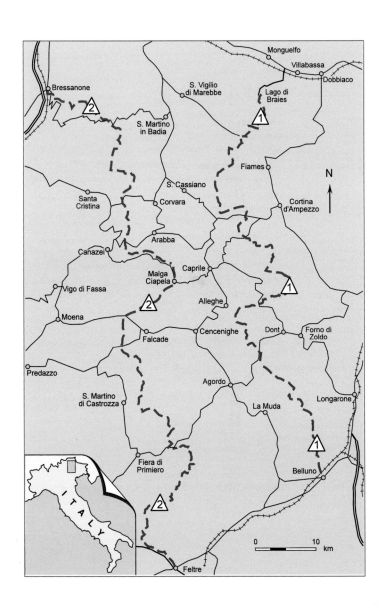

MOUNTAIN SAFETY

Every mountain walk has its dangers, and those described in this guide-book are no exception. All who walk or climb in the mountains should recognise this and take responsibility for themselves and their companions along the way. The author and publisher have made every effort to ensure that the information contained herein was correct when the guide went to press, but they cannot accept responsibility for any loss, injury or inconvenience sustained by any person using this book.

International Distress Signal
(To be used in emergency only)
Six blasts on a whistle (and flashes with a torch after dark) spaced evenly for one minute, followed by a minute's pause. Repeat until an answer is received. The response is three signals per minute followed by a minute's pause.

The following signals are used to communicate with a helicopter:

Help needed:
raise both arms above head to form a 'V'

Help not required:
raise one arm above head, extend other arm downward

Note: *mountain rescue can be very expensive – be adequately insured*

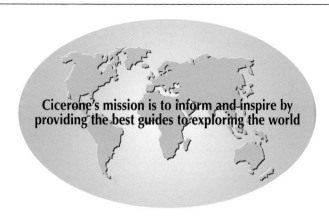

Cicerone's mission is to inform and inspire by
providing the best guides to exploring the world

Since its foundation over 30 years ago, Cicerone has specialised in publishing guidebooks and has built a reputation for quality and reliability. It now publishes nearly 300 guides to the major destinations for outdoor enthusiasts, including Europe, UK and the rest of the world.

Written by leading and committed specialists, Cicerone guides are recognised as the most authoritative. They are full of information, maps and illustrations so that the user can plan and complete a successful and safe trip or expedition – be it a long face climb, a walk over Lakeland fells, an alpine traverse, a Himalayan trek or a ramble in the countryside.

With a thorough introduction to assist planning, clear diagrams, maps and colour photographs to illustrate the terrain and route, and accurate and detailed text, Cicerone guides are designed for ease of use and access to the information.

If the facts on the ground change, or there is any aspect of a guide that you think we can improve, we are always delighted to hear from you.

Cicerone Press
2 Police Square Milnthorpe Cumbria LA7 7PY
Tel:01539 562 069   Fax:01539 563 417
e-mail:info@cicerone.co.uk   web:www.cicerone.co.uk

CICERONE